LEARNING TO LOVE YOURSELF

Finding Your Self-Worth

Sharon Wegscheider-Cruse

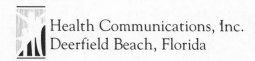

Health Communications, Inc.
Deerfield Beach, Florida

Sharon Wegscheider-Cruse
ONSITE Training & Consulting, Inc.
2820 West Main
Rapid City, SD 57702

Library of Congress Cataloging-in-Publication Data

Wegscheider-Cruse, Sharon
  Learning to love yourself.

  Bibliography: p.
  1. Self-respect.   I. Title.
  BF697.5.S46W43   1987   158'.1   86-32022
  ISBN 0-932194-39-7

© 1987 Sharon Wegscheider-Cruse
ISBN 0-932194-39-7

Published by Health Communications, Inc.
Deerfield Beach, Florida 33442

Dedication

This book is dedicated to:

Myself and the courage it took to claim my freedom . . .

My children — Patrick, Sandra and Deborah who supported me and loved me through the most difficult years of my life . . .

Joe Cruse — His challenge, love and support of me increases and embellishes my self-worth on a daily basis.

A Special Thank You

Mark Worden (Editor)
> My thoughts and ideas have been expanded through the creative artistry of your talents. In addition, it is a joy to work with you. My self-worth has increased by working with you.

Kathleen Johnson
> Your ideas for graphics brings the text alive. Pictures make clear what words often fail to convey.

The Team at Health Communications, Inc.
> Every once in a while a professional relationship is so important that those involved are transformed. That's how I see my relationship with your organization. Thanks for your role in bringing words of hope and help for a waiting and interested public.

Contents

CHAPTER 1
Journey To Self-Worth 1

CHAPTER 2
Parents and Self-Worth 19

CHAPTER 3
New Perspectives on Old Feelings 31

CHAPTER 4
Enemies of Esteem 55

CHAPTER 5
Steps To Higher Self-Worth 77

CHAPTER 6
Intimacy, Commitment & Self-Esteem 93

CHAPTER 7
Guidelines To Developing Intimacy 99

CHAPTER 8
Emotional Needs & Self-Worth 107

REFERENCES 122

CHAPTER ONE

Journey
To
Self-Worth

WHAT ACTUALLY IS SELF WORTH?

Webster's dictionary does not list a word such as self-worth, so let's take it apart and understand each part.

SELF — Personal; Having its own identity; Personality
WORTH — Deserving of value; Useful.

The definition I would give to self-worth would be:

MY VALUABLE IDENTITY
DESERVING ALL GOOD THINGS

How do we know when a person has positive self-esteem, when a person has self-worth, or feels good about themselves? Behavior is a good guide. Yet behavior can be deceptive, because it's possible to act "as if" we have self-confidence, poise and high self-esteem.

There's an old saying: You can't tell a book by its cover. Similarly we can't always tell what's going on inside a person who appears to be perfectly confident and self-assured — the epitome of someone who has a high level of self-esteem.

If we were to tune in on the thoughts of a person with a positive self-attitude, we might hear self-descriptive statements that go like this:

I consider myself a valuable and important person, and I feel that I'm at least as good as anyone else of my age and background. I think I've earned the respect and considera- tion of my peers and co-workers. I sometimes have a positive influence on other people because I try to respect their feelings and don't run roughshod over them. I have a pretty definite idea of what is right, and I'm able and willing to defend these views. At the same time, I feel that I'm fairly flexible, and I'm willing to listen to other points of view without feeling threatened and under attack. I enjoy new and challenging tasks and don't get upset when things don't turn out perfectly right away. I have patience.

What would an interior monolog sound like coming from someone with a negative self attitude? It would be full of pessimism and depression and self-deprecation:

I don't think I'm a very important person or likable person. Actually, I don't see any reason for anyone to like me. I'm really not very good at anything, and I never have been. Others don't pay very much attention to me, and given what I know and feel about myself, I don't blame them. I'm not very adventuresome. I don't like new or unusual occurrences, and I prefer to stick to the known and safe ground. I don't expect very much of myself, either now or in the future. Even when I try very hard, I don't seem to get anywhere. The future really looks hopeless. I don't feel that I have a whole lot of control over what happens to me. It's probably going to get worse.

There are many levels of self-esteem falling between these two instances. For example, at one time or another we have all experienced feelings of inadequacy, anger, guilt, lone- liness, shame and grief.

INADEQUATE

Sitting at the table listening to everyone else, seemingly comfortable and at ease, I feel my inside tighten up? Why does it seem so much easier for everyone else to fit in, make conversation and be part of the group?

ANGRY

Will I ever feel like it's my turn? It seems as though I am constantly putting energy into my relationships. Someone always has a crisis or problem that seems more important than mine. I'm tired of worrying about everyone else and my needs coming last.

DRIVEN AND RESTLESS

Doing well and accomplishing so much doesn't seem to help. When will I feel finished, caught up, satisfied? I'm tired of accomplishing, working, feeling driven. Why can't I stop?

GUILTY

I feel like I should be doing more and be more understanding and helpful. Every time I do something for myself, I feel guilty. Whether it's time, money, or energy, I feel like I should be giving more and taking less.

LONELY

When all is said and done, I really don't feel like very many people truly know me. Most of them only know what I've allowed them to know about me. If they really knew how I felt, what I wanted, and what I worried about, they probably wouldn't like or respect me.

SHAME

Old events continue to haunt me. Just when I feel as though something good is going to happen for me, I remember old events, old feelings and I feel bad about myself again. Will I ever be free of old memories and old shame?

GRIEF

There have been so many losses. It sometimes feels like it's too late to really be happy. Some things cannot change, some relationships can never be. Can I get over old regrets and feelings?

Just when I feel things are going to be better, I pull myself down with old fears, hurts and inadequacies . . .

Sometimes, no matter how I look to others on the outside, what I am feeling like on the inside is 4th class. When my feelings pull me down, I experience low energy 4th class feelings — otherwise known as low self-worth.

Signs of Low Self-Worth

Although we can't always be sure about deducing high self-worth from behavior, we can be fairly certain about some observable signs of low self-worth.

1. Eating disorders (overweight, anorexic, etc.)
2. Trouble with relationships (intimacy, commitments, affairs)
3. Physical problems (chronic health issues, impotence, non-orgasmic.)
4. Drug and alcohol misuse.
5. Workaholism and frenetic activity
6. Smoking
7. Overspending (compulsive shopping to gambling)
8. Dependency on "other" people (family to gurus)

The above behaviors are rooted in our culture and play a

part, in one way or another, in our everyday lives. Eating, working and spending are obviously behaviors that can be useful or harmful. It's our abuse of eating, our abuse of working, our abuse of spending that causes us problems.

We eat for nourishment, but our eating becomes abusive when we overeat until we restrict the scope of our lives, or when we binge and purge, or when we live on high fat snacks.

Compulsive eating, dieting and purging are all ways that we react to how we feel. Take Janet, for instance. When she's hurt or angry, her feelings churn inside. But Janet was taught in her family to be nice, proper and always — *all ways* — keep her feelings under control. Janet's feelings of anxiety result in her feeling driven, rushed and chaotic. She grabs a candy bar or a bag of potato chips and brings her anxiety under control by *feeding her feelings*. In a few minutes, her feelings are manageable and she is able to function again. Janet repeats this pattern several times a day, and carries around fifty extra pounds.

---

*Anxiety Is Simply A Pool of
Undifferentiated Unexpressed Feelings
We Have Accumulated Over the Years*

We work to make a living, and if we're lucky, to attain self-fulfillment. But when work becomes the center of our lives, to the point where we neglect our closest relationships, and even our health, then work becomes self-destructive.

Larry feels that same anxiety in regard to his surfacing feelings. When Larry was a little boy, his father was an extremely powerful figure in his life. Both as a child, then later as a teenager, Larry tried hard to get his father to notice him. He tried grades, sports, and good behavior, yet he never felt noticed, validated, never felt quite good enough. Today Larry is a highly degreed, honored and visible person. He has accomplished much in his profession. Many people are intimidated by his knowledge and power, yet inside Larry feels inadequate and unworthy. His drive to do more and more and still more keep him active and compulsively busy. As a result, the closeness and intimacy he sought with his father in the past is missing in his relationship with his wife and own children in the present. Larry is pushing them away with his workaholism, and his feelings of inadequacy and loneliness keep him "driven" — which in turn intensify the loneliness and distance from others.

We spend money to help us get the things we want and need, but when our spending gets out of control — when we go on shopping binges or gambling streaks — then our spending becomes clearly abusive.

Sandra is the finance officer of a small college. She feels a bit nervous about her work because she's the only one in administration who doesn't have a masters degree. While she's very responsible with the college's finances, her own are in disarray. She keeps her credit cards charged to the limit and goes on shopping sprees and buying binges whenever she feels low. The binges however don't help for long, because Sandra just keeps getting further and further in debt.

The result is that Sandra wears a facade of confidence over her feelings of anxiety. "I just feel so overwhelmed," Sandra confided to a friend. "I know I'm spending more than I make, but it seems to be the only pleasure I get in life." And then she adds, "Besides I never had anything when I was growing up. I owe it to myself. I'm going to be good to myself."

Other behaviors such as smoking and using certain drugs are predictably harmful and we can make choices to avoid these problems. Inevitably our self-abusiveness leads to a vicious circle: Eating, drinking, spending, frantic activity, sexual acting-out are all activities that give us some relief from painful feelings. However, this relief is short term and the original feelings return when the medication (substance or behavior) wears off.

Then we're back on the treadmill, completing the vicious

circle, for now, in addition to the original painful feelings, there are new and increased feelings of guilt, inadequacy, shame, and loneliness. The cure? More booze or drugs. More chocolate fudge sundaes, more chocolate mousse. We work harder, treat ourselves to a big slug of lottery tickets, go on a shopping spree.

We get relief from our pain as long as we're pumped up with excitement. But it's only short-term relief, followed by more painful feelings, and once again we're on the downward spiral of descending low self-worth.

more and more of the same pain increases and behavior worsens drinking, smoking, overeating, using drugs, overworking, overspending, acting out sexually increase feelings of . . . hurt, sadness, guilt, shame, inadequacy lead to more drinking, smoking, overeating, using drugs, overworking, overspending, acting out sexually increase feelings of hurt, sadness, guilt, shame, inadequacy lead to more smoking, drinking, using drugs, overeating, overworking, acting out sexually increase feelings of hurt, sadness, guilt, shame,

As Sandra puts it, "When I start buying things, I feel great. I tell myself, 'Hey, I deserve it. I'm gonna be good to myself for a change!' Then when it's over I've got all this stuff, which is all right, but not that great. And I'm deeper in debt. I go around kind of in a trance with a feeling of doom inside."

As our acting-out behavior increases our inside emotional pain, we need more and more acting-out behavior to get any emotional relief. Our pain increases and our behavior worsens. We continue to hurt ourselves, all the time wondering why we treat ourselves this way and wanting to change.

By this time we have reached a point where we are:

ADDICTED TO:

Alcohol

Drugs

Cigarettes

OR DEPENDENT ON:

Food

Work or power

Possessions

Certain people

The object of our short-term relief becomes like a poison or toxin to us. In these situations substances such as alcohol, drugs, and cigarettes, as well as food, become toxic substances to our emotional well being.

Similarly, we develop toxic relationships. As we become dependent on certain jobs, people, and family members, our relationship to them may become *emotionally toxic* to us. Whatever keeps us from spontaneous, free and authentic emotional response becomes an emotional toxin to us.

Emotional Toxins

Any substance or person who inhibits our ability to feel spontaneous emotion becomes an emotional toxin to us, and produces an environment of toxicity that lowers and keeps low our feelings of self-worth.

First Steps To Greater Self-Worth
The first and most vital step in beginning our journey to

higher self-worth begins with the removal of toxic substances and relationships from out life. This elimination calls for an honest and fearless inventory of our life situations.

An inventory is an honest — stress *honest* — assessment of our strengths and weaknesses. It is giving credit where credit is due, and taking a dispassionate look at some things about ourselves that are hard to admit.

It's important to recognize that we have both positive points and shortcomings and that we are ever-changing. Our strengths can give us the energy and courage to admit our weakness and face them. Therein lies the ability to be able to choose positive changes for ourselves. As we make positive changes, we increase our self-worth.

It is very difficult and in some cases impossible to reach a level of healthy self-esteem while we continue to pollute our body with toxic substances or surround ourself with relationships that sap our energy. Toxic substances and toxic relationships contribute to psychological and physiological stress, intensifying other problems in our lives, making us less capable of making decisions that promote self-worth.

It's hard to grow something (someone) healthy and beautiful in a garbage can. The garbage has to go before growth can happen.

The higher the self-worth, the stronger the conviction that one is worthy of one's fight to live and to be happy. Self-worth, then, can be seen as a basic personal need and a requirement of mental health and sense of well being.

Before any journey of trying to build or raise self-worth, it is important to be aware of what is blocking current self-worth. Most often we arrive at the path of growth by way of either restlessness (wanting something) or pain (wanting to get rid of something).

First Law of Self-Worth

Before moving ahead and raising our self-worth, it is necessary to become fully aware of our present reality and the forces of our past which have held us back.
You can't give energy forward and backward at the same time.

There Are Three Giant Steps to Take if We Want to Develop High Self-Worth . . .

1. Remove the toxic substance or behavior.
2. Look back and make new choices about old messages and feelings.
3. Develop new behaviors and feelings that enhance a budding new growth of self-worth.

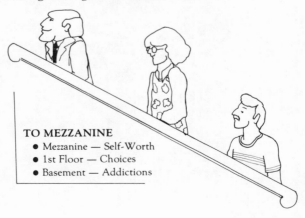

TO MEZZANINE
- Mezzanine — Self-Worth
- 1st Floor — Choices
- Basement — Addictions

Self-Worth Is A Choice, Not A Birthright

Is this heresy? Some may say that my stating that self-worth is not a birthright reveals a negative attitude. To me, it's not negative, it's just simply a belief formed by my past experiences with both clients and friends. Many people were born into families and to parents who themselves were not given healthy doses of self-worth. This lack is passed on from generation to generation.

A child from an early age on experiences the world in relationship to self. To the child, the world reflects back an image that helps the child grow to define itself. If the world (parents, family, friends, teachers) presents the child with a picture of that child's worth, the child feels worthy and acts in a manner to increase the worthiness.

Far too many children were born into families where parents were poorly prepared to give kids the care and attention needed for healthy growth. Some parents were too busy establishing their own worth and place in the world. Other parents were children themselves.

Such child-parents want children, because, they think, children will give unconditional love. Gloria, a mother at sixteen, found this to be true — up to a point. When her daughter Judy Kay was two years old, Gloria became upset because Judy Kay was growing independent and didn't appear to need her mother as much as she used to.

Gloria decided to have another child. "Judy Kay just doesn't need me as much as she used to," Gloria complained. "She doesn't make me feel loved any more." Some of our parents came through the Great Depression and World War II, when they experienced the insecurity of poverty, homelessness and imminent death. The values acquired during these years seemed alien in a time of widespread prosperity that followed WWII.

Each generation then became busy living up to the needs, wants, wishes and rules of the preceding generation. Instead of a child fully appreciating the gift they are, they become busy trying to fit into a family already established. The tendency is to get the approval of the already established adults, rather than explore the gift and surprise inside of each special child.

For many children, especially those born to parents who are unsure of their own worth, there is a family need for them to grow up too fast. This has been called "the hurried child syndrome." In a culture that inflates the value of fast cars, fast foods, instant gratification and nano-second computer speed, there's a tendency to hurry childhood along.

Parents, eager to get their peewee leaguers and mini-twirlers in uniform, take a competitive stance toward growth and development. "Your kid took his first step at 11 months? Hell, mine walked at nine months and was jogging a quarter of a mile at 12 months. And throw a football? You should see this kid's arm!"

Instead of the delights of childhood, the hurried children experience the onerous responsibility of childhood. Instead of celebrating playtime, choices, possibilities, and joy, the time of childhood became a time of performing on schedule, learning rules, taking on responsibility and figuring out how to belong and do things right.

Parents loved you when you performed right. And if you didn't, well . . . You were a failure as a person. Rejection and abandonment, overt or unspoken, were everpresent threats, consequences of failure.

Childhood became painful instead of joyous, responsible instead of carefree and a devaluing of our own needs, wants, and wishes took place instead of a prioritizing value. Self-worth stayed fixed at a childhood level. Trapped like a fossil ant in amber, self-esteem had no opportunity to grow. The feelings around this phenomenon were buried.

VALIDATING THE SELF IN CHILDHOOD

A major contributor to whether or not worth is high or low tends to stem from whether children were given messages that affirmed or validated their existence, their choices, their talents, their ideas, their plans. If these parts of themselves were not validated, children seemed to feel less important or valued than those around them.

Imagine for yourself a large basket given to you at birth. During your early years, you collect learning that gives you energy, hope, skills, desire, and good feelings about yourself. We'll call those messages "flowers." You also collect messages that make you feel inadequate, small, guilty and afraid. We call these messages "garbage messages."

Look at the following messages and assess what you are carrying around in your basket.

Garbage Messages

(Messages that make us feel bad and unloved)

- Don't say anything if you can't say something nice (Hide true feelings)
- Family business is private business (Don't trust)
- Work first, play later (What you do is more important than who you are)
- Boys don't cry (Men should always be strong)
- Women shouldn't get angry (Women should cover up angry feelings)
- Don't speak unless spoken to (Spontaneity is wrong)
- Don't talk about sex (There is something wrong with bodies)
- You made your bed, now lie in it (There is no room for mistakes)
- Anything worth doing is worth doing well (Strive for perfectionism in everything)
- Money doesn't grow on trees (Watch whatever you spend)
- You can do better (What you are doing is not good enough)
- I told you so . . . (You should have listened and did what I said. I am right and you are wrong)
- Don't hang your dirty linen in public (Don't talk and don't ask for help)
- Blood is thicker than water (Family loyalty comes first whether or not it is deserved)

Think about some of your own rules and messages you brought from the family you lived in. How many of them made you feel an increased value about yourself? And how many of them made you feel bad about yourself? Let's look at some positive messages (flowers) that make people feel better about themselves:

1. I'm really proud of you today.
2. That was a really good idea you had.
3. Keep up the good work.
4. You are a very special person.
5. Good for you!
6. You seem to have a lot of good ideas.
7. You'll probably learn a lot from that mistake.
8. It's a pleasure to work/play with you.
9. I like you just the way you are.
10. It's okay to have a lot of feelings.
11. Sometimes tears are refreshing.
12. I'm sorry. You are right.
13. I'm happy when I'm with you.

This book is all about honestly assessing what we are carrying around in our basket and deciding what we want to get rid of. The second half of the book will tell us how to refill our basket with the positive energy of choice and affirmation that will increase our self-worth.

A term often used today is "alienated self." This term simply means that one lives each day reacting to the outside world. This includes partner, family, job, friends, television, and world events. The alienated self does not feel at home in the world, always feels out of place, uncomfortable and anxious. The alienated self goes through life emotionally numb.

Yet at the same time, one remains connected to the "inner self." In the inner self each one of us sorts information, events and feelings that are unique and distinct for each person.

In a sense, the inner self is like our own private computer keeping our pertinent information in storage to be available to us when we can best use it.

It is such a wonderful possibility and system that one wonders — How does a person arrive at the state of being disconnected from their own emotional experience, unable to call upon emotions and feelings to advise and guide? How does the alienated self become an emotionally numb automaton?

To begin with, many parents teach children to repress or swallow their feelings:

- A little boy falls and hurts himself and is told sternly by his father, "Boys don't cry."
- A little girl gets angry at another child who breaks her toy and mother is quick to say, "Don't be angry, it's not nice."

- A child gets all excited about a parade coming down the street and a parent cautions, "Don't get so excited and make so much noise."

Emotionally repressed and stoic parents tend to produce emotionally repressed and stoic children, not just by rules alone, but also by their own example. The child finds spontaneity and emotional freedom giving way to what is "proper," "appropriate," socially acceptable, and one's personhood takes another step backwards. A giant step backwards.

A child in this environment begins to fear "feeling and emotions" and tries to develop ways to control feelings. What is then felt authentically gives way to what is proper to feel and "reality" becomes distorted. Instead of feeling what we feel, we feel what is proper to feel.

The Denial Lifestyle

The possibility of denying our true feelings and our truth is a common problem for children who lived in troubled homes.

As we ignore our inner experience (that which we feel and experience), we disown part of our truth. Our reality therefore becomes distorted and we cannot see our situations clearly.

Statements of a distorted reality tend to minimize the seriousness or possibilities of a situation. We tend to view things *as we choose*, or *as they suit us*, rather than the way they actually are.

Statements Of A Distorted Reality Are:
"Things aren't that bad . . ."
"Things are better than they used to be . . ."
"I'm willing to settle for . . ."
"I can't . . ."
"It's someone else's fault . . ."
"If only you would . . ."

"He, she, it, or they made me feel this way . . ."
"It's hopeless . . ."
"Fix me, I can't help myself . . ."
"You made me be like this . . ."
"I'd be all right if only you . . ."

Keep this in mind:

To grow in self-worth, we must give up the fantasy of our memories and the convenience of seeing our past as all good or all bad.

If we only have all good memories, we will stay in the "myth of the perfect childhood" and we will continue to stay divided from our true self. The myth of the all-bad childhood will keep us stuck in a blame frame and again keep ourselves from using our inner self and experience to help us grow forward.

Self-Worth is a Choice, Not a Birthright

The first major task we will experience in this book will be to make some tough choices, and one of the toughest will be to look for the truth in our growing-up years and find our own sense of reality. Some people say, "Why look back? Why dredge up situations and feelings that are old and forgotten?! Why reopen the wounds?"

The most important reason to look back and examine our early years is this: While the situations and feelings might be old, *they are not forgotten.* They live in our attitudes, thoughts and feelings and affect our day to day current relationships and choices. One of my strong beliefs is "recover or repeat." *What we do not resolve from our growing-up years and early relationships with our families, we will have to resolve with our current relationships. (Mate, friends and children.)*

There is indeed healing power in making choices, and there is a healing power in reality — even in painful reality. But first we must go back and discover what was real and what was myth.

CHAPTER TWO

Parents
and
Self-Worth

It is important at the onset of this chapter to make it clear that the purpose is not to blame the low self-worth of an individual on that person's parents.

Often parents themselves were not given healthy doses of self-worth. Their own parents may have suffered poverty, persecution, oppression, prejudice — and even abandonment. They may have been poorly educated, barely literate. Or chronically ill. Or physically handicapped. Still, we can assume that when they became parents themselves, they tried to do the best they could for their children.

Even though the "best" sometimes was counterproductive, most parents still loved their children. Unfortunately, they just didn't always have the tools it took to give the child an atmosphere that promoted the development of high self-worth.

Every childhood had its storms and stresses. Every child experiences varying degrees of misery and unhappiness and disappointment. Nevertheless, we all somehow grew to adulthood. All of us can recall painful times. We suffered losses — real losses — of pets, friends, or family members. School was a mixed blessing because it gave us opportunity for growth, yet it also insured failure. After all, there were only five places on the cheerleading team. And eleven starters on the football team.

For two years a teenager named Susan drove her parents crazy practicing cheers during every waking minute around the house. She was shattered two years in a row when she missed making the cheerleader team by one vote. Now 35, she reflects, "It was the biggest humiliation of my life. I still look back and get a sick feeling when I think of losing. My closest friends were cheerleaders. But I just wasn't popular enough."

There were attitudes and beliefs in the homes in which we grew up that hurt us. Some of the happenings may have made us feel unacceptable, inadequate and isolated.

Nicolas, for example, recalls abandonment. His father left his mother when Nicolas was five years old. When his mother remarried, his step-father insisted that Nicolas be placed in a military academy. For the next 7 years Nicolas saw his mother once a year. His family was the Academy — strangers who were paid to house him.

And John, now 83, remembers the greatest failure of his life: "I loved school, and when I finished the eighth grade, I wanted to go on to high school. No one in my family had ever done that. The problem was I had to go stay in town." John was born and raised on a homestead in Camas Valley, Idaho. "My parents arranged for a place to stay, and I got a job at the store so I could pay for my keep. But I was a ranch kid, and the town kids made fun of my beat-up ranch clothes. I only lasted a couple of days, then I took the next wagon out of town." All these years later, John still feels a keen sense of humiliation and failure.

Very few of us ever reach adulthood without some kind of psychic scars. However, now that we are grown, we can begin to see things as they really were. Our parents were not the all-powerful, all-wise, strong and omnipotent people we saw them as when we were children. They were ordinary human beings with human abilities and human failings. They had problems of their own — problems which were probably not too different from some of our own problems. While our parents may not have given us what we needed, they probably have done the best they could with the knowledge, understanding and financial resources that they had.

In other words, our parents were not full of unmitigated, unrelenting malice. They are not the villains in the melodrama of our past.

UNFINISHED BUSINESS & THE ADULT CHILD

Our purpose now is to explore what we did and didn't get and identify our "unfinished business." Then we today, as adults, can finish up this business, get our needs met, raise our own self-worth, and get on with life.

Low Self-Worth tends to be part of the package when one has come from a family where expectations are rigid and unreasonably high, where people have rigid rules and where emotions have not been valued. People from such families stop developing emotionally at an early age. It's like their emotional life stays immature — juvenile, or even infantile — while the rest of the child grows, matures.

We sometimes refer to this condition as "emotional retardation." These children develop and sometimes even overdevelop intellectually and physically. Emotionally, however, they are still children. Children, no matter how old they are. These children are often referred to as "adult children."

Outside, they appear to be mature adults. They have adult responsibilities. They live adult lifestyles. Yet inside they suffer the vulnerability of a child. Outwardly they tend to be competent and successful, but inside their hearts and souls suffer.

My experience with people who have a sense of low self-worth [LSW] is that they are always "getting ready to get ready for when." I like to say to them, "The show is on and the rehearsal is over. Life is here now." This is an important concept, because LSWs are usually thinking about the time they will become who they are going to be. They believe that only then will they feel better and happier. They seem to be waiting for an event or a person who is going to impact them in such a way that now they can be happy.

It's important to come to know that this is all there is. There isn't something to attain, there is only something to be.

Happiness isn't something you strive for like an academic degree. And it isn't something that comes in a neat package marked "happiness," nor does it automatically come when you meet Mr. or Ms. Right.

Happiness involves facing and accepting reality *as it is* and going with that flow. And this means accepting certain physical and sometimes financial circumstances on oneself and others.

Happiness comes in many different forms. Sometimes it's very intense, sometimes it's barely perceptible. *We're often happiest, in restrospect, when we're least preoccupied with the question of happiness.*

There isn't something to do or something to accomplish in order to be happy and satisfied. It's being, not doing . . .

Adult children live in expectation. As children, they believed that when they got out of their homes, they would be independent, free from the oppressive, heavy-handed supervision of hopelessly square parents. Emancipated, they could manage their own time to suit themselves. They would find new and exciting people to be with.

One thing for certain: They would find the magical kingdom and be happy. They would certainly not be like their parents. No way.

One of the major expectations is that there will be a minimum of unhappiness, a minimum of unpleasant feelings. I think this comes about as a result of blaming parents and others for the pain and unhappiness in one's life. Once a person is on his own, so to speak, those extraneous malevolent influences are no longer around, so one expects life to be more pleasant, less stressful, happier. Perhaps part of happiness is being able to endure the pain of life, the disappointments, the unhappiness, to live through it and get on with other business, instead of wallowing in misery indefinitely.

These thoughts, feelings and ideas were formed during childhood. Instead of listening and trusting our inner selves, many got caught up in the expectations of family, school, friends and the media. Television is an important (and sometimes subtle) source for many of our expectations — happiness come with a name-brand cologne, femininity in pantyhose. Advertising is notorious for playing off our low self-esteem — as shown years ago by Vance Packard in his book *The Hidden Persuaders*.

Becoming Acquainted With Your Inner Child

Inside of me lives my very special mentor, recorder and teacher. It's "my inner child." Sometimes a person is quite familiar with their inside self (the repository of self-worth) and sometimes the inner child is unknown. In this sense, we can be strangers to ourselves.

Much distress, fatigue, hurt and loneliness could be understood and eliminated if we had more understanding and working knowledge of our inner child. Such understanding could help us encounter each other in relationships and also give us help in finding our own worth as people.

Once upon a time, each of us were children. It was an important time and today the impact of that time remains with us. Oftentimes, in our adult way, we try to ignore our lives as children, discount the importance of the learnings of that time and ignore the lessons available to us. The lessons learned in childhood affect the way we think, feel and act today. Some of those lessons enhance or interfere with the way we have learned to interact and the way we have learned

to love and be loved. Such feelings may even be a significant part of our fatigue, inability to relax, headaches, chronic anxiety and depression.

Think about the child that was you . . . What happened?
1. Did your child die?
2. Was the child in you outgrown and cast aside like old toys or clothes?
3. Did you abandon your child?
4. Or did your childhood self become irrelevant, lost, empty of meaning?
5. Is the child who you were alive and doing well?

Each person carries with them the feelings and attitudes brought with them from childhood. Some of the low self-worth environments included homes where:

The Child Needed To Become "Grown Up Too Soon . . ."

These are homes where for whatever reason the parents were unable to provide emotional safety and comfort for the child. These are homes where one or both of the parents were or are dependent on alcohol and drugs and the parent's preoccupation with their own needs takes precedence in the family. The children learn to care for themselves emotionally and sometimes even physically. The older ones feel responsible for the younger ones and the childhood is a time of responsibility and fear.

The Child Was Expected To Be "Perfect . . ."

Perfectionism is created in the child by the parent's holding back acceptance and affection until the child earned it. The child responds to this demand by trying in an over-serious effort to achieve physically, intellectually and socially. The child never achieves enough to satisfy the parents or themselves. . .

The Child Was Constantly Pushed, Pulled and Preached To . . .

This is a child who was the recipient of a parent who constantly directed, suggested, supervised and talked endlessly with the child about direction, plans, reminders, goals, etc. The child eventually gives up all self-directed action and relies on outside stimulus in most areas of his/her life. Eventually, the norm for the child is to forget, procrastinate, resist, and experience apathy and listlessness. This child has a hard time becoming a self-starter.

The Child Who Reflected The Parent's Anger . . .

This is the child who is a true victim in the family in which they grew up. This is the child of a parent who has few tools with which to express his feelings of anger and hurt. In this type of troubled family, a defenseless child becomes the target of the parent's anger. In these homes, we see physical and emotional abuse. Unfortunately, some of the forms of anger are subtle, such as sarcasm, insults, and rigid rules.

The Child Who Is A Victim of Parental Neglect . . .

The most common form of child abuse in this country is

emotional neglect. In addition to the physical forms of neglect, countless children have suffered from emotional neglect. It often occurs because of the busyness and preoccupation of the parents, often afflicting children of prominent and economically successful people. It is also a common occurrence for children who have grown up with alcoholism in the family.

Neglect can be caused by anything that deprives a child of his parent's loving attention and affection. It can be work, busyness, absence, death, etc. One of the major difficulties about emotional neglect is that it is elusive and gives a feeling of emptiness, rather than something specific that can be pointed at, weighed, measured and clearly described and understood. Neglect is hard for children to put into words, and this difficulty is continued in adulthood. People report a vague, restless emptiness rather than something that can be described or understood.

Often as children and as adults, people report feelings of numbness, uncertainty, emptiness. Instead of being able to describe episodes that were painful they are most likely to say "nothing too bad" ever happened. This offhand comment can be an important clue that something critical was missing in childhood and that neglect was taking place. If there was a mother or father who somehow did not make themselves available in times of emotional need, neglect did in fact take place.

The Child Was Exposed To "Crazymaking" Behavior . . .

"Crazymaking" behavior is when two messages that are contradictory are given at the same time. Example:

— I want you to feel free to follow your own dreams, remembering that we are all counting on you to carry on the family business.

— I love you just the way you are, I only give you advice and suggestions because there are just a few things you could change.

Crazymaking Double Messages

From my mentor, Virginia Satir, I learned about double

level messages. She states, "The troubled families I have known all have handled their communication through double-level messages. The result is a feeling of 'craziness'. Something is wrong."

"Crazymaking" behavior is when two messages that are contradictory are given at the same time. Example:

— I want you to feel free to follow your own dreams, remembering that we are all counting on you to carry on the family business.

— I love you just the way you are, I only give you advice and suggestions because there are just a few things you could change.

— I want you to go out and have a good time. I don't mind being lonely.

— I know you love me, but you just don't know how to show it.

— We'll have lots of time together; just not now.

— I can take care of myself quite well, but I wish you were around more.

— I'm fine — don't worry about me. I just don't feel good.

— We'll always take care of you and there is plenty to go around. Things are just a little tight right now.

People in our lives want credit for their good intentions, but don't want their disappointing behavior to count. We learn early not to expect that good things will really happen. No matter what is said, no matter how many smiles — in the painful family things did not feel right. What you saw and what you heard often did not match with how you felt.

We even learn how to behave with ourselves in double message ways.

— We overeat, then we diet.

— We drive two miles to the exercise club to walk two miles around the track.

— We take a vacation and spend considerable time calling home to check on things.

Consistency, focus and living in the present are styles that are seldom learned in the painful family.

Usually in crazymaking situations the often stated message is one of goodwill, support, concern, and care. The second, often unspoken message is more indirect. Usually it's something we don't want to hear or face. Often, it's an action . . . forgetting special days, missing a cab, arriving late, acting confused or fragile. It's the behavior that makes it hard to trust the words that sound supportive and caring . . .

For many, childhood was not a time of building high self-worth and confidence. It was a time of feeling grown up too soon, afraid and unsure of oneself. In the next chapters we will explore some of the painful hang-overs and then move on to ways of celebrating ourselves and raising our own self-worth . . .

WHY IT IS IMPORTANT TO MORE FULLY UNDERSTAND OUR FEELINGS

For many children, the early years of life were filled with frightening and painful experiences. Perhaps a child had parents who rarely responded to the child's need to be touched, held and comforted. Or perhaps the parents yelled and screamed at the child, displacing their own frustration and anger onto the child.

A very painful method of control that parents sometimes use in order to communicate with the child is instilling guilt and fear in the child to make them "behave." And sometimes parents are just neglectful and indifferent. Many a child can tell painful stories of the parent who continuously criticizes and makes fun. There is also the parent who makes demands and expectations that no child can possibly fulfill.

A young child simply does not have a conceptual knowledge of his own needs nor does the child understand why the parents are the way they are. They may have been broken or mistreated children themselves. They suffered lost childhoods, they experienced humiliation, grief and dashed expectations. But young children don't know the secret parts of their parents' pain. They don't have the skill of empathy. Children, busy trying to learn their own way around in the world, fail to see that their parents are lost souls themselves.

At times the fear, guilt, anger and hurt that a child feels become so overwhelming that the child, in order to survive, disowns the part of themselves that can "feel." It's a necessary defense mechanism. In order to survive and in order to keep functioning, the child escapes from his inner knowledge and feeling. The child denies and buries the inner child.

These old feelings become frozen into the body, barricaded behind walls of muscular and physiological tension. The child then goes on to develop protective behaviors (compulsions such as food, alcohol, cigarettes, sex). To medicate this internal pain, the system of compulsion (behavior) and repression (inside feelings trapped) are set up — often without full knowledge of the person. This then becomes the source of Denial and Delusion on our lives.

Our feelings are a sixth sense, the sense that interprets, arranges, directs and gives understanding to the other five. Not to feel — to be emotionally numb and unresponsive — is to be deprived of more balanced perspective of reality. Not to feel is to shut off the possibility of being truly connected to others. Feelings are the common denominator of all people.

Because so much of reality depends on the knowledge of our feelings, we walk through life both confused and overwhelmed if we are not aware of our own feelings and the feelings of others. Understanding the language of feelings is the key to mastery of ourselves. With increased knowledge, one can become free of negative feelings so that higher, more creative energy can be released. As more creative energy is released, more feelings of fear and pain subside. This is the other side of the vicious circle — it's a self-reinforcing cycle of positive feedback.

When you suffer the emotional pain that everyone occasionally suffers, you will be drained of energy and feel hurt and hopeless for awhile. This is natural. If you allow yourself to fully experience and feel the natural stages of hurt, anger and pain, without avoiding the reality — without denying it — you will resolve and heal quicker and more completely. Your energy, creativity, and productiveness will return. The process of solving emotional problems throughout life makes possible real growth and development. The issues of childhood constantly reappear as conflicts in our lives. If we remain open, we grow. If we are closed and defensive, we waste our energy and never reach our potential. Our early goal is dependency, our next goal is independence. The last goal is mastery and freedom.

. . . Understanding and Feeling Feelings Is Freedom . . .

FORGIVENESS

Forgiveness is a gift we give ourselves. It implies that we admit that we do not know the complete circumstances of the people who have had an impact on our lives. We do not possess the omniscience to be able to say "Dad should have been able to pay more attention to us kids" or "Mom shouldn't have been so uptight all the time." Forgiveness acknowledges that we do not have the knowledge or the wisdom to sit as judge, jury and executioner over people who may have hurt us in the past.

Forgiveness is a choice. We choose life for ourselves and others when we forgive.

1. We relieve ourselves of the burden of carrying around hurt, anger, pain and loneliness. Healing happens for us.
2. We give someone else the freedom to live their life (or sometimes rest in peace) and work out all their own behaviors, feelings and consequences.

Forgiveness
is
the healing gift we give ourselves

CHAPTER THREE

New Perspectives On Old Feelings

UNDERSTANDING FEELINGS

Some people may be baffled when I talk about understanding feelings. "What's there to understand?" they ask. "I know when I feel good, and I know when I feel bad. What's so complicated about that?"

If emotions were simply a matter of feeling good at one time or bad at another, then it's true — there wouldn't be much to understand. But as we've seen, our present feelings are laden with an emotional history, a history set down during childhood and carried into the present.

Keep this in mind:
At times the fear, guilt, anger and hurt that a child feels become so overwhelming that the child, in order to survive, disowns the part of themselves that can "feel." It's a necessary defense mechanism. In order to survive and in order to keep functioning, the child

escapes from his inner knowledge and feeling. The child denies and buries the inner child.

Thus, even though the child tries to escape the feelings, bury and suppress them, the feelings remain. We are, after all, emotional beings, as well as rational beings, and we are hardwired for emotions.

So the feelings formed in childhood become frozen — encapsulated in time, so to speak — and carry over like a time capsule into the present. It's true that we know when we feel good and when we feel bad, but it's also true that we deny many of our feelings, deny them because

● . . . we fear them
● . . . we're ashamed of them
● . . . we think they're bad
● . . . we think they're abnormal

As I indicated in the last chapter, our feelings constitute a kind of sixth sense, a sense that interprets, arranges, directs and gives understanding to the other five. In a literal sense, not to feel — to be emotionally numb, frozen, closed off and unresponsive — results in an unbalanced view of the world and of other humans. The person who tries to vigilantly control and suppress emotions shuts off the possibility of being truly connected to others. Such a person is not truly human, *for feelings are the common denominator of humanity.*

GETTING IN TOUCH

Psychologists, counselors and therapists have placed a great deal of emphasis on the importance of getting in touch with one's feelings. What does it mean to get in touch?

First of all, getting in touch means becoming aware that we have feelings. Getting in touch with our feelings means becoming acquainted with our subterranean emotional life. And it means learning to accept our emotional life as a natural aspect of ourselves, not something to be feared or shunned as repugnant.

When we're not in touch, we're like sleepwalkers,

moving through life in a trance, jolted now and then to a confusing wakefulness. Trembling and fuzzy-minded, we're overwhelmed by our own emotions and perplexed by the emotions of others.

Understanding the language of feelings is one of the keys to self-mastery.

When we're in touch with our emotions — when we have a grasp of the language of feelings — we have indispensable tools for resolving emotional problems throughout life. The ability to resolve these problems makes real growth and development possible.

Inevitably, as we've seen, childhood issues keep coming up in adulthood and are the source of much adult conflict. If we remain open to change, open to understanding the language of feelings, we have the potential to grow. If we opt to keep sleepwalking, waking fitfully now and then, our energy dissipates and we remain something more than automatons, but less than human.

There's a drive in most of us to move from dependency to independence and then on to mastery and freedom. Let's see how understanding emotions gives us a new perspective and enhances our ability to fulfill our potential as thinking, feeling, acting persons — fully human beings.

REMEMBER: *Freedom lies in understanding feelings and being able to act on that new understanding.*

ANGER

Anger is a word we apply to a wide range of feelings . . .

- Anger can be as simple as a minor irritation.
- We frequently feel angry when we're frustrated or when our plans are thwarted.
- Annoyances may be barely noticeable at first, but if

annoyances continue, they can generate considerable wrath.

- Sometimes we experience rage — sometimes called blind rage, because it seems uncontrollable.
- We feel a form of anger when we're disappointed and let down — most often it takes the form of resentment.
- When we're angry, but don't want to make a big deal out of it, we use a euphemism. "I'm really teed-off."

Anger is frequently a response to being hurt or suffering loss. Even so, we may not recognize it as such. For example, if someone says, "I never get angry," they may really not know how to recognize their anger. Or they are very much aware of their anger and want to deny it, because they've been taught that these kinds of feelings are socially unacceptable, bad, or wicked. Sometimes people want to deny their anger because they fear it — they fear that they'll unleash a torrent of rage, go completely out of control, cause some kind of irreparable harm.

"I have to sit on my anger," explains Gordon, a 55-year-old retired policeman. "I was trained to stay in control, and frankly I've been worried at times what I'd do if my anger got out of hand." He adds pointedly, "I've been around guns all my life but I don't keep a gun in the house. Anyone who's been in law enforcement will tell you that most firearm homicides take place in the home, and most shootings take place when there's been drinking during a family dispute."

It is important to recognize the feeling of anger because anger is a *natural* emotion. It's normal to feel angry at times. Anger becomes problematic when, on the one hand we pretend it doesn't exist, or on the other hand we *use* our anger to manipulate and intimidate others.

There are two steps in understanding anger:

1. First, get to know your own anger better — in all its varieties. See how it affects you, how your breath quickens and your pulse pounds. Feel the flush of blood to your face and the tension in your hands, legs,

neck and stomach. Notice how your facial muscles change, get a good look at yourself.

2. Learn to direct your anger *in an appropriate way to the appropriate people.*

Expressing anger is a natural, healthy response and is necessary to keep oneself healthy and in balance. Sometimes feeling angry can be unpleasant. Blood pressure will often rise and the heartbeat accelerates. But this tension needs to be released outwardly — and appropriately — or it needs to be acknowledged. If not, it can, in some instances, go inside to fester and irritate. To hold anger back and dwell on it adds to the hurt that caused it.

There is a difference between a person who releases appropriate anger when injured and a person who seems to be chronically angry and venting most of the time. A chronically angry and bitter person often feels short changed in life and blames others for his problems. This is using anger as a defense and a rationalization for blaming others.

This is not healthy or appropriate anger. Specificity is a good measure of appropriate anger. It is tied to an event or situation that can be specifically described.

Assertive behavior prevents aggressive behavior. Assertive behavior protects one's rights and feelings, whereas aggression attacks someone else's rights and feelings.

While many people would like to become more assertive, they often don't realize that assertiveness is a skill. And they sometimes confuse assertiveness with aggression. What's an appropriate assertive expression?

1. Telling someone when you're angry, and why. Share the anger with the true feeling behind the words. Don't be evasive or apologetic or humble when the emotion you feel is anger. At the same time, do not explode and become irrational.

2. In situations where it may not be safe to express your anger, you can release the pent-up feelings with a friend or a therapist trained to facilitate this release. It is important to correctly acknowledge the situation so that words, motion

and sound are important vehicles of release.

Note: Kicking the dog, running 20 miles a day, or constantly rearranging the furniture are *not* appropriate.

Learning to identify anger is a major part of the growing and healing process. Many people mistakenly call this feeling hurt, sadness or guilt, when it is truly anger they feel.

Staying stuck in anger can keep people depressed, tired, hurt, frustrated, confused, isolated and fearful. And ruminating bitterly about past injustices, hurts, and conflicts takes a lot of energy that could be used for promoting personal growth.

Over time, anger that is pushed down produces rage. Rage becomes more generalized as it builds up, while anger is more specific, more easily communicated and more easily healed. One of the benefits for expressing honest anger is that oftentimes, the person is then able to feel relief, be more understood, and sometimes be more accepted. If expressed properly, anger can actually clear the way for intimacy.

However, anger which is expressed in an unclear, disguised or veiled way can make a situation worse. For example, take the case of Hank and Celia, a young couple who've been married for two years. During his bachelor days, Hank regularly met his two older brothers in a restaurant every Saturday morning for breakfast and man-talk. After breakfast they might take in a ballgame or car show. This regular Saturday morning ritual continued after Hank and Celia returned from their honeymoon.

As one might expect, Hank's Saturday bull sessions didn't exactly thrill Celia. She and Hank both worked full time and weekends were the only times they had for each other. Because she loved Hank and enjoyed his company, she wanted to spend as much time with him as possible — talking, playing, and making love. She also wanted some help with the housework . . .

When Hank continued to spend six to eight hours every Saturday with his brothers, Celia felt angry, hurt, left out and jealous. It seemed to her that Hank cared more for his brothers than he did for her.

As you can see, this was a situation primed to explode.

Celia had grown up in a family where she learned that anger was a dangerous emotion, never to be directly expressed until the situation became so intolerable that you blew your stack. So how did Celia express her angry feelings? She nagged. She complained. She made sarcastic comments.

Instead of telling Hank she felt lonely and wanted to spend time with him because she loved him, she said things like, "I suppose you're going out with your brothers again" — in a tone that thoroughly indicated her disapproval.

She complained about the money he spent, made disparaging comments about his brothers and insinuated that he was too weak to break away from his family.

When these tactics failed to keep Hank home, Celia sulked and cried and withdrew into an angry silence. To get even with Hank, she started to refuse his sexual advances on Saturday night.

How did Hank respond? He fought fire with fire. When she nagged and complained, he became defiant and aloof. A gulf of resentment grew between them.

Desperate to improve her marriage, Celia sought counseling. She learned a better way to express her anger. Instead of expressing her anger through tears, sarcasm or withdrawal, she learned to acknowledge the true nature of what she was feeling to herself and how to express her feelings to Hank in a non-accusatory and caring fashion.

Like most of us, Celia had been raised to believe that a confrontation always had to be nasty and unpleasant and negative. But it *doesn't have to be that way*. A confrontation — even an angry confrontation — can be a well-thought-out, dispassionate, lovingly firm statement to someone we care about. Our goal is to make our point, maintain our self-respect, and not demolish the other person. We want to point out how a certain behavior is causing trouble, we offer possible solutions, and we express our commitment to make that change easier.

Instead of sarcastically accusing Hank of being an inconsiderate oaf who cared nothing for her feelings and who still needed the approval of his loutish big brothers in order to feel like a man, Celia said, "I feel angry because . . . ," and she then told her husband about her feelings of loneliness and isolation. She assured him that she loved him and that she didn't want to completely separate him from his brothers, but she would like to spend at least two Saturdays of the month with him.

What would they do? Talk, picnic, watch T.V., clean house, make love or visit her family for a change. They could compromise and take turns. Most of all she wanted him to know that she wanted to spend time with him because she enjoyed his company.

How did Hank react? At first he got defensive. He was expecting more of the same old accusations. But Celia didn't react negatively when Hank bristled. She restated her concerns clearly and immediately, she gave specific examples, and she didn't demand that Hank cave in to her demands completely.

Hank and Celia's marriage is much better now. Hank says, "I always knew Celia was ticked off about the time I spent with my brothers, but I always thought it was because she was jealous and selfish and possessive. I don't think I ever realized how much she really cared for me until she stopped nagging."

Learning how to openly express both her negative angry feelings and positive loving feelings helped bring Celia the intimacy she yearned for.

Breaking out of anger and rage often means having to break those patterns from childhood that said, "You must stuff feelings rather than fully express them." Expressing anger will help a person get "unstuck" and be able to go and feel other feelings.

Blocks To Expressing Anger

1. Dependent people are afraid that being angry will prove them unlovable. They are afraid people will

reject them or abandon them. They struggle half-heartedly and tend to whine and complain rather than get angry and use that energy constructively to work toward resolution. They waste much energy and often feel depressed and apathetic.

2. Controlling people tend to intellectualize their anger and remove all feelings from it. They confuse the issues, look at every possible perspective and verbalize or avoid instead of feel. They stockpile so much anger that occasionally they vent out irrationally. Their fear of "loss of control" is often justified since they have so little consistent healthy expression.

3. People pleasers are people who often disguise their anger. They hint around about being angry, all the time smiling through clenched teeth. Often, the feelings manifest themselves as physical complaints. Headaches, muscle tension and stomach upsets are all signals of held-in anger.

Hints For Expressing Healthy Anger

1. Be silent and let all the feelings of anger rise to the surface . . .
2. Validate and appreciate yourself inside for being able and willing to feel the truth of the anger you feel . . .
3. Express the feeling of anger as honestly and as soon as you can to the appropriate person/people . . .
4. Appreciate yourself again for being honest and direct . . .

I felt angry when you . . . .

but its okay now.

GUILT

Guilt is the feeling of being unworthy, wrong, stupid and sorry. Oftentimes guilt is the result of holding anger inward to the point of turning it against oneself. Overly guilty people tend to wallow in their negative feelings as a way of punishing themselves and getting some relief from the guilt they feel. A common trait the guilty person feels similar to the angry person is that they have difficulty directing feelings toward the source of the long held-in anger. As time goes on, the person doubts his worth and turns more and more negative energy in on self, reinforcing the feelings of guilt.

This is particularly true if there have been conflicting relationships between persons or in families. At some point, one person calls a halt to the conflict and decides to seek help or make changes. This might be when one person goes to counseling or an alcoholic seeks treatment. This seeking of help and ending of the games is a confrontation to all the games and dishonesties in the family or relationship.

When the person who is seeking help and change begins to change and begins to develop a feeling of self-worth, it is often threatening to those who do not choose to get help or change. They will frequently blame counseling or therapy for the changes in the other and accuse them of not caring, or not being willing to enter the same destructive power struggles.

Sometimes the person who has sought help is so unaccustomed to feeling better about himself that he reports feeling guilty when accused. It's important to know that these feelings are not feelings of true guilt. They are actually feelings of "recovery guilt" otherwise known as "anger." It's so scary to be angry about growing self-worth that the temptation is to call this feeling guilt. It needs to correctly be labeled as anger and expressed as such . . . Every person willing to work for it deserves high self-worth and all the good things that come with it.

Every Person Willing To Work For It Deserves High Self-Worth and All The Good Things That Come With It.

Feelings of guilt can get a hold of us and direct energies inward as it punishes, often in confused, illogical and uncontrolled ways. Our memory then becomes selective, focusing on only the times we violate a higher value, or caused someone pain or suffering.

Evidence of former accomplishments and goodness

become vague, harder to remember, while the transgressions remain fresh and alive in memory. Recalling only the guilt, we then continue to feel bad about ourselves. We seem to become dependent on and addicted to unfulfilling jobs, unhappy relationships and punishing life situations.

Two situations seem especially guilt-producing: when one feels anger towards parents and/or children. Somehow these two groups seem to generate a great deal of anxiety and uncertainty in dealing with angry feelings. It's important to remember that there will be times when the most appropriate feeling to have toward parents or children is healthy anger.

When we are appropriately angry with our children, we teach them boundaries and respect. As we respect ourself and set boundaries about how we are willing to be treated, we teach them that it is expected and appropriate that they have a right to set boundaries around themselves. As we teach our children how to express and receive and learn from anger, we lay a foundation for how we will treat each other as adults and hopefully grow into mature friendships with each other.

Parents are another matter entirely. We sometimes mythmake that our parents are always correct people and will always accept us and know best about most things. However, reality is that parents — all parents — are simply people who happened to have children.

Repeat:

Parents are simply people who happened to have children.

And that fact alone doesn't mean that they are more responsible, knowledgeable or caring than people who didn't have children.

A child that is not taught in childhood that anger is a healthy expression often feels guilty as an adult for expressing natural angry feelings towards parents. That child as an adult often harbors resentment towards parents as he sees that they withheld love and support at a time when the child needed it most.

The anger that couldn't be voiced in childhood still seeks expression and yet as an adult today, the person is still afraid of doing anything for self, because of a feeling that would be voicing anti-parent feelings which will only increase guilt. If one is living in constant fear of hurting parent's feelings, life becomes a painful replay of a confused childhood and affects every other relationship one has with a fear of expressing anger or hurt.

It is crucial to emphasize anger resolution between the child and the parent because the *unresolved* fear and anger of our early relationships color our adult relationships in the present — whether we know it or not.

It is also important to acknowledge that there is such a thing as appropriate guilt. This kind of guilt is healthy and is a signal that we have offended or wronged another person or ourself in some way.

Appropriate guilt makes us feel uncomfortable until we have made amends or restitution to the wronged person. To deny responsibility for hurting someone would only reinforce the guilt. The best way to relieve yourself is to accept the blame for your actions, to apologize and to repair the damage you have done. This has a remarkable way of easing inner tension and making everyone including yourself feel better.

To Deny Responsibility For Hurting Someone Only Reinforces Guilt. The Best Way To Relieve Yourself Is To Accept The Blame For Your Actions, To Apologize And To Repair The Damage For What You Have Done.

To break out of a pattern of a lifetime of guilt is difficult, but not nearly so difficult as continuing to live a guilt-ridden life.

Consider the saga of Carol. Carol, a 20-year-old young woman seeking her own career, felt guilty each time she tried to leave home. At the same time, she felt trapped. She was a physical and emotional wreck. Her mother was "sickly" and Carol's father relied on her heavily as his "princess."

As Carol grew older, she hungered for a relationship, for relief from the pressures and needs of her parents. She eventually was able to move to another city, but only after many tearful sessions with her parents.

Carol moved 800 miles away, but the guilt lingered on. Mom needed Carol for help, support and company. Dad needed Carol to be the mainstay of the household and to help with Mom. Even though Carol lived 800 miles away, she went home at least once a month and dutifully called home every two or three days.

The men Carol dated fell low on her list of priorities. She had other obligations, other demands on her time and emotions.

After her third loss of a male relationship, Carol went into therapy. There she learned that she had missed much of her own childhood, that she was enmeshed in her parents' marriage, and that she was, in a sense, being used emotionally. In order to develop as a person, she needed her own time, space and distance. But when she tried to get what she needed, she felt emotionally punished by her parents.

Gradually Carol developed an understanding of her own needs and became aware that her parents had a responsibility to fulfill each other's needs.

Carol moved again, this time to a New England town she had always longed to visit. Before leaving, Carol explained to her parents why she had the need to get so far away. She also set up specific boundaries for contacts with them.

With a great deal of guilt-free courage, Carol set about living her life.

Hints For Getting Rid of Unhealthy Guilt

1. Stop pretending to yourself and everyone else that you don't feel or that your feelings do not matter . . .
2. Remember to always be honest with your own needs. You are not obligated to meet the needs of others.

That is their obligation. You owe yourself loyalty to yourself.

3. Remember, only you can know what's best for you. You do not need to meet anyone's standards or expectations other than your own.

4. Believe in yourself and your feelings and accept yourself just as you are. You are quite okay just the way you are.

5. Honestly, ask yourself . . .

What do you want for yourself in this life???
What are you doing to get it???
What is in your way???
Who put it there???
Why have you waited for a crisis to force you to act???
Where are you going from here???

Remember this essential fact:

No one owns you — no matter what the relationship. You are not here on this earth to fulfill the dreams, wants or wishes of a parent, a mate or a child. You are also not responsible to protect any other person from facing their own consequences or realities. You are here to exist, to develop and to grow and be responsible to and for yourself. In the bigger picture of things, it would be well if you also contributed to making this world a better place to be because you passed through it.

My Journey Is My Journey

SHAME

Shame is different from guilt. Guilt is an offense that is specific and is committed against self or others. Shame, on the other hand, is a generalization that is unclear. It is a feeling of being worthless and not as good as other people. In shame-based families, people feel as though their existence simply does not matter. It is not necessarily good or bad. It just doesn't matter. When we feel shame, there is really nothing we can do. We simply feel as though we are worthless and nothing really makes a difference.

Sometimes people call on institutions to reinforce shame. Churches, schools, authorities become a symbol of what is good and proper and people set up these authorities as being good and themselves as bad if they do not meet the criteria of the authority. Shame is an attitude and a powerless situation. Shame cannot be healed. It can only be changed into guilt and then guilt has possibilities for behavior change.

Guilt has to do with behavior . . .

- Lying to a friend
- Getting drunk and having a car accident
- Stealing money from a parent
- Constantly picking arguments with a partner
- Ignoring the needs of others.

Shame is a condition of low self-worth. Guilt is a response to an event. Guilt that accumulates (unexpressed) becomes shame. Instead of feeling badly in regard to an event, those feelings accumulate until the events are forgotten, and the person just feels like a bad person. For example, if one feels guilty about never going home to visit family and old friends, eventually one feels like the "bad" person in the family. That "bad person" feeling is shame.

Sometimes a person chooses not to practice the religion of the family and feels "bad" about it. Or a woman might have sex outside of marriage, get pregnant and have an abortion — and as a consequence feels like a "bad person."

These are some typical instances of shame.

Shame has to do with feeling worthless . . .

- Feeling too short
- Feeling not as smart as others
- Feeling unattractive
- Feeling unimportant
- Feeling undesirable
- Feeling stupid

DEPRESSION

Depression, like guilt, often occurs when anger is turned inward. It takes energy, responsibility and excitement to make the world an attractive, healthy place to be. The person with anger bubbling inside has very little healthy energy to give to self, others, or the world. When a happy person and a depressed person look at the same object, one sees the best in it and the other sees the worst in it. The depressed person sees, in people and the world, a reflection of how they feel inside. They tend to concentrate on missing people, inside emptiness, unfulfilled dreams, problems, worthlessness. Energy turns against the self.

Here are a couple of common examples:

- Christmas approaches. Ken and Martha are eager to see their five children. A week before the holidays, one child calls to say she won't be able to make it home for Christmas. Ken accepts this change in plans with some disappointment, and he gets on with life. Martha, on the other hand, frets and fumes and cries during Christmas dinner about the one child who couldn't be there. Martha makes everyone very uncomfortable and cuts short the good feelings among the rest of the family.
- Steve wishes his father could
  — hug him
  — be interested in his career
  — accept him and love his wife

Over time, Steve's father does accept Steve and his wife and becomes interested in Steve's career. Yet Steve reports feeling unloved because his father is still uncomfortable about hugging him.

Steve and Martha tend to be sad and feel unloved because they can't have exactly what they want. In their disappointment, they miss the joy of what they do have.

People who have had a loss feel a normal and healthy sadness. Their sadness is mixed with anger which they express. Sometimes there is even a healthy expression of grief. Those who experience a loss, but do not go through the stages of anger (expressed) and grief (expressed) accumulate events. The feelings around unexpressed anger and grief turn to non-specific depression.

After a while the person even forgets about the actual event and just know they feel depressed. The longer it goes on, the further away the events become and the more difficult it is to find a resolution and return to energy that is healthy and filled with life.

Directing energy outward is the first step in confronting depression. For a while just paying attention to this body energy will help. Making a commitment to keep moving and reawaken the body in regard to activity, sleep patterns, and involvement with people. As the body returns to using some outward-directed energy, one feels more life returning. When the body starts to feel again, it's important to look for clues of guilt or anger. Beginning to express even the smallest feelings of anger or irritation will further wake up the depressed person.

Minor depression may respond to simple body changes and the depressed person starting to talk about irritations and disappointments. The more deeply depressed a person is, the more likely they may need to receive counseling to help uncover the anger and guilt they have been working so hard to avoid.

However, keep in mind that some forms of depression have biochemical origins and may result from poor self-care habits — such as subclinical nutrition from eccentric eating habits (too much, or too little, wrong stuff) caffeinism, sedentary lifestyles, stress, and so on.

Moreover, some people have been found to have a genetic predisposition to depression and become depressed because of neurotransmitter malfunctions or because of seasonal light fluctuations. Once these forms of depression are ruled out, then one can focus on depression of psychological origin, depression fueled by anger.

One way out of a depression fueled by anger is to find and unleash the anger that pulls the person inward. Appropriate expression of that anger may help lift the depression.

One warning: Expressing feelings does not automatically "cure" feelings. In other words, venting your rage to the universe may make you feel better for a while, but by itself, ventilation is no panacea, no cure-all for depression.

What does seem to be most helpful is having someone — a therapeutic presence — who can listen to your depression without discounting it. Someone who can identify the anger if it's there, or who can guide you to better self-care, if it's indicated. Someone who's well-enough acquainted with depression to be able to tell whether you've got the blues, an allergic reaction, a side effect of some medication, seasonal affective disorder, PMS (or other hormonal dysfunctions).

Insight and disclosure of feelings do not automatically make depression disappear. People often learn to ventilate their feelings, learn to express their anger, fear and resentment, and they have loads of insight. But nothing seems to change. Something else is probably needed, and that is the expectation that the individual will have to *do something*, besides emote and be insightful in therapy. Without this expectation, troubled people can easily end up becoming therapy junkies, skilled jargoneers, proficient in expressing emotions (you want anger? I got anger . . . Grrrr!) (You want tears? Take this [the sound of water . . .]) and adept at reaching profound insights about why they do this or why they feel that.

Consider this: When a therapist encourages the expression of emotions, there's sometimes an assumption that those who are in the vicinity will act in a caring and therapeutic manner. In fact, the opposite is probably most often true. It may not be wise to be emotionally expressive in some situations. It may not be safe. It may not be discreet, and discretion, as Shakespeare's Falstaff reminds us may be the better part of valour.

GRIEF

Grief is the normal response to loss. When we suffer a significant loss there is a whole bevy of feelings accompanying this loss. There will be anger, hurt, guilt, terror, emptiness, sadness, helplessness. Grief is the clustering of the normal feelings that accompany any major loss. We may be referring to the loss of a person, such as in death, divorce, or an estrangement of someone dear to us.

Or we may feel grief about
- The loss of a childhood (the child who grows up in a home where emotional and sometimes physical needs were not able to be met, ie, an alcoholic family).
- The loss of health (someone struggling with the diagnosis of a disease).
- The loss of a dream (finding out that your child will not fulfill the dreams you had for that child).
- The loss of a hope (the promotion just isn't going to be coming).

In short, there are many causes for natural and normal grief.

To grieve is normal. An abnormal grief would be the refusal to feel all the necessary feelings to move through the process or to refuse to accept the support that is offered. To work through grief, it is necessary to let all the feelings surface and then to express them. It's a process by which we admit the reality of the loss and then move on to live without it, rather than to preoccupy ourselves and those around us with constant reference to it. Griefwork is a difficult venture. It's our willingness to live on as decent, caring and responsible human beings, no matter how hard a time we've had, or what a significant loss we've had.

As we've seen, loss and grief have many aspects. Felicia, a 40-year-old housewife, had to work through multiple losses, multiple griefs in just a short period of time. She lost her husband to another woman, which meant that she had to cope with divorce, the hassles of living single, the reduced income — all the while feeling like a living part of her had been ripped from her gut — seventeen years of marriage, of memories good and bad.

"It was a blow," she told her counselor. "At times I really felt as if I'd have been better off dead."

But Felicia gained courage to face her losses and to move beyond them. It wasn't easy. It meant new friends, a job, and perhaps hardest of all — it meant taking a hard look at Felicia, taking that fearless and honest inventory, so that she could get past the grief, anger and resentment and get on with doing something positive for Felicia.

We will learn to live in the present with things as they are and open ourselves to the experiences of the world. We will do all this, even though we have had losses.

We detach from the past to make room for the present. We do not detach, however, until we have taken responsibility to express our feelings about it. Then we get on with it. We note there are many people around who will help us if we only reach out. We stop rejecting the many just because we can't have exactly who we want. We give up emotional infancy and in the trade find emotional maturity and some sense of comfort and fulfillment.

Life is a mixed bag and we all suffer some losses:
. . . A happy childhood
. . . The health and physical power of youth
. . . The fantasy that one will be powerful and live forever
. . . Financial security
. . . Children leave home
. . . Sometimes a loved one goes away and does not come back
. . . A job we really valued
. . . Divorce

Some losses come too soon and some seem unfair, but life is partly learning how to adjust to loss and coming to terms with the perceived unfairness. Ultimately, of course, life itself is lost.

Grief, then, is not weakness, nor is it a punishment. Grief is a psychological and emotional fact of life. Learning how to adjust and work through it is a necessity. It's an honorable and valuable emotion. Working through grief is therapeutic.

Grief provides insight and wisdom. You can begin to see what is important and what is not important. You are able to feel energy in your feelings. Such self-awareness will help you grow toward wholeness and come to a deeper understanding of yourself.

From Elisabeth Kubler-Ross, we have learned about the natural stages of the grief process:

1. Denial (This can't be happening to me)
2. Anger (Why me, why now?)
3. Bargaining (Maybe if I tried harder, maybe if I change, this wouldn't happen)
4. Depression (Helplessness and surrender)
5. Acceptance (This is the way it is, I will accept and make the most of what is happening.)

During this time there are many kinds of body changes. These, too, are normal. They include:
● Tightness in the chest
● Rapid breathing
● Headaches

- Loss of appetite
- Sleeplessness

In time, if the stages of grief are faced and felt, the sense of acceptance leads to inner healing. There will always be some feelings of sadness and loss, but these feelings will be integrated into our reality, not control our behavior and energy levels. We will begin to live again.

Ready to live again, we make note of that fact that we do not return to "our old self." When we have suffered a significant loss, we come out of it as a different person. Depending upon the way we respond to that loss, we are either stronger or weaker, either healthier in spirit or sicker.

If we have not gone through all the grief stages and asked for help when we needed it, there are probably many internal battles still raging inside. Others who have grieved in a healthy way understand that while they have endured a significant loss, not everything has been taken away. They realize that while life will not be the same again, many good things in life remain — good relationships and the infinite variety of life itself.

Eventually the dark clouds begin to break up and occasionally for brief moments rays of the sun come through.

There are many more painful feelings we could explore. The following feelings are often buried deep inside. Take a few minutes, read these feelings and allow your own thought and feelings to surface . . .

- Jealousy
- Hatred
- Moodiness
- Frustration
- Gloom
- Worry
- Embarrassment
- Discouragement

Make a commitment to yourself that you want to free yourself of old emotional baggage so that you can then free yourself of the behavior that keeps those feelings medicated or buried.

And above all, remember

Feelings are the common denominator of humanity
and
Understanding the language of feelings is essential
to self-mastery, independence and freedom.

CHAPTER FOUR

Enemies
of
Esteem

The journey to high self-worth begins the same way for all of us. We need to ask ourselves honestly:

- What do I feel?
- Why do I feel that way?
- Have I felt that way before?
- What event or person is linked to that feeling?
- What have I done about this feeling before?
- What can I do about this feeling now?

The way to the highest self-worth is by becoming more aware of your own feelings and expressing them in a straightforward, and appropriate, manner. Only you know the person — the inner child — within you. Your goal is to free the child. To attain that goal, you must be fiercely honest with yourself. You must become open to the language of feelings — your own feelings and those of others.

In so doing, you will become responsible to all aspects of your self, all dimensions of your own unique personhood. You will end the fragmentation of the alienated self, and become a whole, integrated person. You will have the satisfaction of knowing truly who you are. In this process of growth and awareness you will find yourself becoming free of emotional baggage and unfinished business, free of obstructive clutter from the past. You will be able to like yourself without explanation or apology. You will achieve a sense of high self-worth, firmly grounded in self-trust and self-knowledge.

On paper, of course, it all sounds so easy. In reality, we are frequently faced with many barriers and pitfalls on our journey to self-esteem. And the main obstacles arise from our own behavior, our own self-stultifying habits and psychonoxious compulsions. In medicating, evading or escaping our emotional pain, we become fugitives from life. Instead of moving toward self-fulfillment, we are mired in behavior inimical to growth.

ALCOHOL, COCAINE AND OTHER ADDICTIVE CHEMICALS

Alcohol and other mood-altering chemicals are dependable feeling-medicators par excellence. They can be counted on to give us predictable mood change. Many things influence moods: Weather, movies, church, poetry, news, cartoons, pizza, and so on. But nothing alters moods as quickly and predictably as alcohol and other chemicals — whether prescribed drugs like Valium, Tranzene and Librium, or illicit "recreational" drugs like marijuana, PCP, amphetamines, and cocaine. There's an enormous market for chemical mood-controllers of all kinds.

For many people in this culture (perhaps a third of the population), regular use of alcohol is an ingrained cultural habit. For many, the regular use of alcohol — the "domesticated drug" — provides a relatively cheap, pleasant and comfortable mood change.

One of the valued mood changes is the fairly predictable feeling of relaxation and warmth. For the occasional user of alcohol, these changes are not terribly important because the user has drug-free ways of feeling relaxation and warmth as well.

Yet for another group of people (about one in every seven individuals), alcohol is highly valued because it does wonderful things for them. They "love" the way it makes them feel. It becomes important to seek the use of alcohol because a "love" affair has been started. The person feels much better with the use of alcohol than the way he feels without it.

This "love" affair is also present with the use of cocaine, prescription mood-altering medicine and other drugs. In time, the good feeling that comes from the use of these chemicals becomes increasingly important to the user, and a dependency is formed. Freedom of choice gives way to feelings of strong urgency to enjoy again and again the pleasurable rewards of use. Natural good feelings are sought after less, as the predictable good feelings from the chemical are sought.

In his booklet, *The Romance: A Story of Chemical Dependency*, Dr. Joseph R. Cruse has described the main conditions for the development of chemical dependency: There must be a susceptible host, a toxic, poisonous agent, and a permissive environment. "The basic mechanism by which alcoholism or other chemical dependency develops in a susceptible person is unknown," writes Dr. Cruse. "But some sort of a *romance* develops between the *agent* and *host* when the natural chemicals of a susceptible person's brain meet certain mind- and mood-altering chemicals (drugs) such as alcohol. A love affair begins . . ."

For the person who has never known how to get good and pleasurable feelings in a natural way chemicals sometime provide the first good feelings they have ever experienced. The idea that it is possible to get good feelings from something that is predictable becomes a very seductive and important idea. The chemical becomes more and more important to the user.

As freedom and choice lessen, the person uses alcohol or drugs much more frequently and these episodes of use bring with them problems. The chemical becomes important to the user.

As freedom and choice lessen, the person uses alcohol or drugs much more frequently and these episodes of use bring with them problems in relationships. Sometimes behavior is less than desirable and sometimes it is outright embarrassing and emotionally painful.

As these episodes continue and problems in the relationship intensify, feelings of remorse, sadness, anger and fear emerge. Over time, then, we use chemicals not merely to bring a predictable feeling of pleasure, but rather to bring relief. We use chemicals to quiet the painful feelings now brought about by the chemical use itself. As you can see, a vicious cycle has been set up:

- Use to feel good
- Use more and more to feel good with negative consequences.
- Use to feel better from the feelings of the negative consequences causing increased negative consequences, etc. etc. etc.

The use begins to run roughshod over other emotions as they are constantly medicated and held deep inside.

Reliance on chemicals for changes of mood stagnates natural emotional life, and our feelings become increasingly deadened. In time, the highs and good feelings are not as high or as good any more, and the lows are much lower. The end result is a chronically depressed emotional life where it becomes "normal" to feel bad.

In my book *Another Chance*, I have described in detail the addiction spiral and the erosion of personal potential that takes place during the course of chemical dependency. Let us not be coy about addiction. Given the right combination of susceptible host, toxic agent and permissive environment, addiction — physical dependency on the drug — will occur. And with it, predictably, there will also occur the erosion of one's emotional, physical, social, volitional and spiritual potentials.

Most of the time, by the time a person has reached this kind of consistent use, it is very difficult to stop using without some kind of professional care. Fortunately, there are many types of treatment and help available for the chronic alcohol or drug user. Good treatment programs recognize the need to recover the feeling life of the user, and thirty-day treatment programs unlock and release long-term emotional pain and give the tools to continue to use one's own natural pleasures and highs to get the most out of life.

EATING DISORDERS

Eating disorders take a variety of forms, ranging from extreme obesity to binging and purging and anorexia. Why do people develop eating disorders? Is obesity the result of some unresolved emotional conflict from the past? How about anorexia and bulimia — do people (mainly women) become anorexic because of emotional problems rooted in the past?

At present, we have no pat answers as to why people develop eating disorders. Some forms of obesity can result from glandular malfunction. Many people gain weight when taking certain kinds of medication.

Eating disorders can result from unresolved underlying emotional conflicts, or they can be *intensified* by emotional conflicts carried over from the past. And obviously the coping with stresses originating in the present can also play a role in exacerbating eating disorders as well as other dependencies.

It's also clear that in many cases eating disorders have much in common with other addictions. Recent research has disclosed that while the degree of obesity depends on environmental factors, heredity also plays a strong role.

As with other compulsions and addictions, the most successful programs dealing with eating disorders have been those that focus primarily on behavioral change techniques, allied with self-help psychology and peer-group support.

Regardless of the origin of eating disorders, for most of us when conflicts, past and present, create an intolerable level of frustration and internal tension, foods tend to be a comforting substance that gives temporary relief to the distressed person.

In a natural way, food is always intermingled with interpersonal and emotional experiences. Our psychological associations with food have been set up at birth. The special smells and tastes of foods are strong emotional triggers. We do not merely have a salivary reflex in anticipation of a meal, but we often have complex emotional responses. We "love" certain foods (such as ice cream), and we "hate" other foods (such as brussels sprouts) — not merely because of the taste, but because of the associations we have with the food. Ice cream, for example, has always been provided as a reward or special treat in an atmosphere of relaxation and fun. Vegetables, on the other hand, often have an element of coercion associated with them — "Eat your vegetables!" was a stern command. No fun times with brussels sprouts. All business.

Likewise, cookies and desserts have typically been our rewards for being good, candy for special treats, Thanksgiving dinners and family time — all these special occasions carry an enormous emotional freight. There are three major complications with people with eating disorders:

1. Metabolic alterations caused by the extreme presence or absence of fat.
2. The use of diuretics, diet pills, laxatives, vomiting, etc. to alter the fat.
3. The numbing of emotional pain, which results in a person not having their emotional self available to them.

OBESITY

Obesity is usually defined as a 30% excess of fat above ideal body weight. The obese person is predisposed to hypertension, gall bladder problems, diabetes, degenerative joint disease, enhanced surgical risk, impaired functioning sexually and psychosocial disturbances.

In addition, obesity greatly limits one's range of activities, often leading to a relatively isolated sedentary life. Fat people tire more easily. They suffer more foot problems because feet weren't made to carry the excess poundage. When you're fat, your legs chafe when you walk, and you have trouble getting in and out of chairs, cars, theater seats, public transportation, airplanes, and so on. Bicycles and rowboats are risky, so you seek your leisure and comfort elsewhere — often at home in front of TV, with a snack at hand.

Food is a great comforter. A comfort-food urge can strike anytime, but certain occasions can make us more vulnerable, like when we're feeling tired, cranky, lonely. Solitary evenings are prime time for comfort-food attacks. When someone is with you, companionship is nurturing. However, when you're alone, one smell or sight can be a soothing reminder of love and security. Food has a way of putting us in touch with memories of people, places and things. In painful or difficult times, it is reasonable to recreate things that made us happy in childhood.

Different people have certain favorites that bring comfort:

- Pot roast, mashed potatoes and gravy
- Grilled steaks on a warm, balmy night

- Chocolate anything
- Ice Cream
- Popcorn
- Hot dogs with mustard

Notice how memories and feelings are instantly stirred. Food textures evoke certain feelings. Creamy foods soothe as they slide down easily and require little effort to chew. Some have called these "nurture foods." Other foods that are crunchy, such as popcorn and peanuts, help us to let off steam as we work our way through a handful or bowlful.

Sweets and starches have been shown, through clinical research, to have a calming effect on the brain. This is because they increase levels of serotonin, a brain chemical which acts as a natural mood calmer. So when you dig into silky, slippery noodles (tranquility in a bowl), or an equally soothing scoop of ice cream, you are medicating yourself against stress.

ANOREXIA

Anorexia Nervosa has been labeled the "Starvation Disease." It's a mysterious disease, frequently striking young women who are high achievers and excellent performers. While no one cause is known for this illness, anorexics are likely to come from families with these characteristics:

1. Poor communication within the family: There seems to be a lack of freedom about expressing feelings. Only good feelings are accepted.
2. Preoccupation with physical appearance: Usually the family is talking constantly about body size, fitness and appearances.
3. Family members are most valued for their accomplishments: Very often there are clear expectations about the child needing to perform and do well in most areas of their life.
4. Alcoholism in the family: Anorexics are likely to come from a family where the norm is to avoid feelings. Very often alcoholism and depression are common occurrences.

The anorexic is able to get some mood or emotional change by controlling her body. Very few feelings are expressed in the family of an anorexic, and the mood change that comes from the ability and exhiliration of controlling one's body is at least some form of "high."

Anorexics fall into categories. Restricters severely limit their food intake until they are far below their normal weight. Bulimic anorexics, however, will starve themselves for a period of time, and then binge and vomit. The bulimic seems to be more impulsive, more despairing and sometimes more suicidal.

Whether we are talking about obesity, anorexia, or bulimia, we are talking about people using food or lack of food as a medium for salving or comforting the feeling of life.

We should also keep in mind that no one theory can account for all kinds of eating disorders. For example, it's tempting to state unequivocally that unresolved emotional conflicts lie at the root of all food disorder, but the latest research shows that eating disorders, like alcoholism and other dependencies, are influenced by genetic factors. Obesity, for example, has a strong genetic element, but at the same time, the degree of fatness depends on environmental factors, some of which may include emotional conflicts and the like. Similarly, there's more and more research indicating that bulimia and anorexia have a biological origin, with emotional and psychological components.

Whether or not we know everything we need to know how to treat these diseases, we do know that the eating or non-eating compulsions must be stopped before any emotional healing can take place.

The first step to dealing with an eating disorder is to make the effort to try and correct it. If overweight, *Overeater's Anonymous* is one of the best programs to both lose and maintain weight loss. If anorexic or bulimic, seek out one of the co-dependency programs that specializes in eating disorders.

The most successful programs dealing with eating disorders have been those that focus on helping the individual work through pain from the past while using behavioral change techniques, allied with self-help psychology and peer-group support.

The combination of techniques is critical because experience has shown that working on emotional conflicts alone has not been too fruitful in dealing directly with the compulsion.

The classic example of this, of course, is chemical addiction, which has a strong genetic loading. In past years there has been a tremendous battle fought to get chemical dependency recognized as a primary disease rather than as a symptom of an underlying, unresolved emotional conflict. No longer do knowledgeable therapists try to treat alcoholism while the patient is still drinking. Abstinence is taken to be a pre-condition — not a by-product — of therapy.

If there are no treatment programs in your area and you cannot leave the area to seek help, consult a family physician and be as honest as you possibly can about your eating habits as well as the circumstances that are going on in your life. Get the best help you can. You deserve it.

SMOKING

Smoking has become a major devastating disorder. Tobacco and nicotine poisoning is a polite and subtle destroyer of emotion and people. Rarely is there a divorce, arrest, lost job, car accident or hangover that can be specifically tied to cigarette smoking. However, cigarettes kill quietly, in a friendly kind of way. They destroy the emotional life, then very often the physical life of the smoker.

We all know about the destructive body consequences of smoking. Lung disease, emphysema, cancers, heart disease, embolisms, etc., are all diseases linked to smoking. We also know that birth defects, particularly still births and sudden infant death syndrome, are significantly higher in babies of smokers.

What we have not been as aware of is that nicotine and smoke are effective medicators of feelings and emotion. A sure test of the medicinal capability of cigarette smoke is the return of free floating anxiety as soon as a smoker tries to quit. Over time, the many natural feelings that have surfaced and cried for expression have been medicated away by smoking. Eventually, all the connections to those feelings may have been forgotten. The person just feels numb or blank in regard to many emotional experiences and memories. When there is an attempt to quit smoking, all the old buried anxiety returns. Anxiety is simply "undifferentiated feelings."

In order to fully recover self-worth, it will be necessary to stop smoking and let the old feelings surface. Through exploring all the old anxieties and feelings, it will become possible to claim that part of self that has been so long medicated with cigarette smoke. It will not be real easy to give up the cigarettes. They have become a friend — yet a friend with a sting.

For many people, quitting can be quite painless. It is easiest for those who can truly say to themselves "smoking is no big deal and neither is quitting." They just simply quit.

Others may need help, and there are many kinds of help

available. The co-dependent treatment program, listed at the front of this book will help work through the emotions around quitting. There are also specific treatment groups that you may be able to find in your locale.

Smoking interferes with the attainment of intimacy and personal growth. Self-worth is cheated for the smoker. Smoking serves as a security blanket, or insulator, from the world of uncertainty and psychic pain. By turning to cigarettes during times of stress, people are less likely to find the strength within themselves. In a sense, for many people, tobacco is being held on to as a crutch.

Crutches are interesting things. When someone breaks a leg, it's very helpful to use a crutch. But after the leg is mended, we put the crutch away and help the leg return to its full use. Otherwise, the leg's muscles will shrivel from disuse and eventually become so weak and withered as to become useless and always in need of a crutch.

For a smoker, there develops withered emotional muscles. For whatever reason, the smoker has decided to lean on a cigarette to deal with emotional discomfort. And it works for a while. However, the longer the crutch is used, the more the emotional muscle deteriorates and the more fragile the natural response is. Eventually the person becomes emotionally dependent on the cigarette to relieve emotional tension.

There are three main stages that one goes through to give up smoking.

1. It is most necessary to make a decision that one wants to quit smoking and is willing to go through whatever discomfort there is in order to do so. At this stage one makes a decision to set up circumstances to support quitting. This may include joining a support group, attending a formal treatment program or seeking some other type of counseling.
2. The physical phase is when the smoker has to deal directly with the discomfort of nicotine withdrawal. Some go cold turkey, and some withdraw gradually. It

may be discomfort, yet it is manageable tension.
is in a support group or treatment program, this tension is greatly relieved by being able to talk about all
the feelings that are starting to surface. This is a time to
be especially caring of oneself and ask for as much help
and support as you need.

3. This final stage is the time of grief. Refer back to what
   we have already discussed about the grief process. Giving up a habit that has been so intimate requires a
   grieving process. One perceives that one has lost a
   companion, identity and a friend. Time will help. Keep
   remembering that it has been said that the "smoker is
   making love with death."

Break The Chain

of Addiction

INADEQUACY/WORKAHOLISM

Inadequate — Not sufficient
   Not enough
   Less than
   Not equal

Sound familiar? Of course it does. Who is the soul so
self-confident and assured (deluded and arrogant?) who has
not felt for a moment a pang of inadequacy? Even Superman
becomes an inadequate wimp in the presence of Kryptonite!

Feelings of inadequacy can frequently propel us into self-destructive behavior. Even though we may have accomplished great things, many of us are still driven on to do more and more, as if striving to get the notice of some mysterious judge who is ready to say, "That's good, you've done enough."

In homes where approval and praise were given out for jobs done, performance completed, and deeds accomplished, it was very easy and natural for a child to begin to equate their worth with the accomplished task. However, self-worth does not grow with tasks accomplished. Self-worth grows as we learn who and what we are and move in the direction of our own self-love and acceptance.

Many times it seems as if our achievements have a paradoxical effect: They introduce us to more assignments, more responsibilities, more things to be accomplished. And there are times when we get too caught up in *doing* — in accomplishing our tasks — we forget to pay attention to our many other needs and parts. We neglect ourselves, as well as others around us, oblivious to our self-knowledge and best interest.

Stan, for example, has started to realize that something's very much awry in his life. He's been known as a hard worker for years — someone who gave 150 percent. He kept his nose to the grindstone in college, earning an MBA in five years. And he went for two years on his first job without taking a vacation.

The last five years, Stan's wife has succeeded in getting him to take time off from work. But even when he takes time off, he brings along a briefcase full of papers, and like a sneak drinker, Stan sneaks work in during his leisure time.

Stan's job is terribly important to him, and so is his wife. He's been getting feedback that she's feeling neglected, and he's in a quandary. If he doesn't spend all that time at work, he feels anxious. And if his wife is unhappy, he gets anxious.

Trying to keep everything under tight control, he feels as though he's falling further behind. He's often too tired for sex, and when he and his wife do find some time to make love, he approaches it in a businesslike way. Consequently their lovelife is brief, perfunctory and joyless. In fact, their marriage is characterized by a lack of true intimacy. Stan is not only a stranger to his wife, but he is a stranger to himself.

Like Stan, in the driven and busy lives we create for ourselves, we often lose our sense of self-worth.

Frenetic activity (exercise, sports, meetings, classes, jobs, more meetings) drains energy and leaves us feeling physically tired and emotionally numb. Activity, of course, is essential for health and recreation. Yet the compulsively-driven, active person uses activity to numb out feeling.

The workaholic can be a valuable contributor to the community — a hard worker, a dedicated volunteer, someone who gets things done. And society reinforces the workaholic accordingly:

- Dedication means hard work and personal sacrifice.
- The world belongs to the hard worker.
- You've got to get ahead in this world.

In addition to the occupational workaholic we also see other varieties of compulsive activity:

The Homemaker Workaholic

Everything is centered around the house. Meals, decorating, fixing up, changing, repairing, yards. Week-ends are filled with endless "home duties".

The Parent Workaholic

Life is centered around the children. Everything that goes on in this family is centered around children's activities. Holidays, vacations, finances, education are all focused on children's needs.

The Sport Workaholic

Pick the sport!! Golf, tennis, football. Being around a sport addict (active or passive) is a lonely place to be. Preoccupation interferes with relationships, and the self-worth of significant others.

The Professional Workaholic

These are people who somehow feel as though their "profession" and their "specific job" is the most important focus in the whole world. They sacrifice time, energy and relationships just to keep their job, their contacts, and their interests in the forefront.

Workaholism has many faces, but there are some common features of *all* forms of workaholism. Workaholics have faces that:

- Appear tired (especially around the eyes)
- Appear sad often (After all they are experiencing relationship loneliness). There are two kinds of loneliness. One is the absence of physical closeness. The other is having someone you love and care about physically close, but so preoccupied that they are emotionally distant. Both kinds of loneliness are common for the workaholic.

Some other signs of the workaholic:

1. Staying late on the job
2. Never getting done working in the home
3. Working on weekends
4. Always carrying a briefcase or a book to read
5. Rarely absent because of illness or need for a break
6. Often skips or cuts short vacation time
7. Always busy
8. Eats fast
9. Reluctant to delegate
10. Feels responsible to act on every creative idea

Unfortunately, there is not necessarily a connection between working hard and accomplishing much. One study recently showed that computer-workers who took work home to do on their PCs were actually less productive than those who did not.

Any efficiency expert can tell you that there is useless work that goes on every day in most positions. Activity for the sake of appearing busy. Busywork. In fact, too often we tend to think more about how much and how hard we work rather than how *well* we work.

Unfortunately, our culture often places a premium on busywork. Employers HATE to see employees who aren't busy doing something. If you work in a restaurant and there's slack time, you'd better polish counters — even if they've been polished over and over today. If you're in the military service — especially during basic training — and there's some free time, you'd better look busy — otherwise the Sarge'll think you're a goldbrick and you'll find yourself fieldstripping cigarette butts or swabbing latrines. In college some "teachers" put a premium on quantity of work, rather than quality. More than one Ed major has found that it pays to turn in quantities of work rather than small amounts of work of high quality. In short, in many jobs and professions the appearance of work is as highly rewarded as work itself, and meaningless activity is a way of avoiding punishment.

Why Does the Workaholic Keep Driving On and On? It *pays off — see above — and also . . .*
1. To numb emotion.
2. To cover insecurities (work makes one look important).
3. To get thanks and appreciation from others (Fills in for lack of love).
4. To be noticed and liked.
5. Inability to get pleasure from leisure time.

What a wonderful thing it would be if someone would say to us, "Good job done. Now take plenty of time and be good to yourself. Take time to play, to pleasure, to relax. You will still get the things done that you want to accomplish."

Well, probably someone is not going to say those things to us, but we can say them to ourselves. And we can mean it. When we commit ourself to the person inside (child within), who may have missed some of the pleasure and excitement of childhood, that now is the time to make up for lost time, we will also be committing to put work in its healthy perspective.

Alternatives to Compulsive Busyness
Listen to music
Go for a walk
Go swimming
Dance
Read a fiction book
Listen to the trees rustle
Write a letter
Take a bath
Talk with a friend
Play with your children
Tell secrets with someone you love
Watch a candle burn
Pray
Make love with your special partner
Make home-made bread
Build a birdhouse
Look at old pictures
Plan a party
Go to a movie, eat popcorn and hold hands
Play an instrument
Sing
Write down important thoughts to you
Explore a new town
People-watch
Introduce yourself to three people
Call an old friend
Plant a garden or a flower pot
Make presents and give them away during the course of a year.

RELATIONSHIP DEPENDENCY

Perhaps one of the most difficult dependencies to live with and even more difficult to confront is the "people dependency." We are a culture of people enmeshed in each other, and very often a person has not experienced the health and comfort of being an independent whole person. Too often a child goes from being a child into a relationship as a very young person, to a marriage, to becoming a parent without ever becoming a whole individual, without ever having a chance to develop their own potential, without having a chance to explore other aspects of the world. Even if a marriage contract is not present, people tend to be in committed partnerships, still preventing them from appreciating their own wholeness.

Partnering and marriage are very special relationships, and later on in this book I will talk about intimacy and commitment (one of the great fulfillments). At this point, I am referring to unhealthy dependency relationships. These are relationships more developed around need than sharing. Persons in dependent relationships tend to come from families that fostered helplessness rather than self-confidence. This leaves a person vulnerable to developing dependent relationships.

When a person goes to another with the goal of filling a void in self, the relationship quickly becomes the center of his or her life. It offers a comfort that is reassuring and predictable and so the person keeps returning to the relationship for a fix. As this experience repeats itself more and more often, dependency grows. In time, the idea of separation or withdrawal brings a great deal of fear, anxiety and tension.

Separation

Withdrawal

Fear
Anxiety
Tension

A person who is void of his own self-worth strives to fill it with someone else's worth. He draws on the worth of his partner to such an extreme that the partner often feels himself void inside and he in turn looks to someone or something to fill his void. Alcohol, work, food, affairs, power, — all work to fill inside voids. Sometimes one tries to get all needs met from one partner and sometimes one runs from partner to partner to try and do the impossible which is getting self-worth from another. You can see the impossibility. Self-worth can only come from the self.

Self-Worth Can Only Come From the "Self."

Dependent lovers see each other more and more in order to maintain this security they find with each other. When they are apart, they long for each other. Even if they bicker and can't get along with each other, they long for the security of the relationship. To plan to separate or get needs met anywhere by either partner is a threat that brings great conflict into the relationship. How serious the dependency has become is clearly evident when it ends. Since the relationship has been used to cover up so much personal low self-worth, there is disorientation and agony at the end. Often a great deal of anger is expressed. Because the involvement has been so total, the ending of a relationship will expose the exploitation that has been going on throughout the time the couple has been together.

This kind of dependency is not limited to "love relationships." It is also true of friends. Dependent relationships can develop between any two people who seek self-worth outside of themselves. The more self-worth they can take from a friend, the more dependent they will be on that friend. The lower the self-worth, the more friends one needs in order to get adequate amounts of their self-worth. This is not to be confused with the wonderful sharing that goes on between high self-worth friends. Sharing and dependency are two different things.

Signs of Dependency with Lovers or Friends . . .
1. Initiating most of the phone calls
2. Initiating most of the times spent together
3. Wanting to talk about the friendship or relationship more often than the other
4. Feelings of anxiety when not with the other or others
5. Uncomfortable during separation times
6. Concerned or unhappy when the other seems perfectly satisfied and happy when not together
7. Wanting to know everything the other does, thinks and feels
8. Carrying a disproportionate responsibility for the relationship
9. Feeling as though the other's wants and needs are more important than yours
10. Feeling as though you can't make it on your own if you leave the relationship or friendship

It is through our own development as whole people that we find our self-worth that enables us to then choose to be in a relationship with someone of mutual high self-worth and then can share our worth, rather than use each other. Personal high self-worth is necessary before one can enter a healthy relationship.

I like me!   I like you!
I like us!

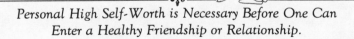

Personal High Self-Worth is Necessary Before One Can
Enter a Healthy Friendship or Relationship.

CHAPTER FIVE

Steps To A Higher Self-Worth

"I want to know and care about myself. I want to feel high energy and a sense of freedom." That's my nutshell description of the essence of high self-worth. High self-worth means also that I am able to:

- Make choices that impact the way I live. I am not a helpless creature drifting passively at the mercy of the winds of chance and the currents of fortune. I am a choicemaker and actively determine my own existence.

- Enjoy my own body. I am a multi-dimensional being —mental, spiritual and physical, and I can take equal pleasure in my body, mind and spirit.

- Recognize and accept that the way I feel about myself inside affects the way I relate to people outside. When I feel positive about myself, I am able to build and maintain positive, life-enhancing relationships. And I am able to relate to people in meaningful and satisfying ways.

- Finally, I know that as I raise my own self-worth, I will feel more integrity, honesty, compassion, energy and love. And I am able to truly experience joy in my life.

All growth depends on a favorable climate, nurturance, and a non-hostile environment. Just as harsh conditions can stunt the growth of a magnificent Sequoia, so the climate— the nurturance and relationships in our lives — can stunt the growth of our self-worth. As we continue this section on how to raise your self-worth, one indispensable factor is necessary:

It will be up to you to surround yourself with people who will support your journey.

It is impossible to raise your self-worth while living around negative people who do not see you as worthy. It is impossible for the self to thrive in a hostile atmosphere where there is little or no acknowledgement or appreciation. Feelings of worth can only flourish in a climate where individual differences are appreciated, mistakes are tolerated, sharing and communication is open, and rules and expectations are flexible. The exciting thing is that there is always hope and possibility because you can learn to make new choices that can change and renew your life.

The Exciting Thing Is That There Is Always Hope
and
Possibility
Because You Can Learn To make New Choices
To Change and Renew Your Life

In the next few chapters I will talk about some of the things we want and how to get them. Each step toward self-fulfillment gives us forward momentum and raises our self-worth just a bit more. Get ready to take very good care of yourself. **You deserve it!**

In case you have some doubts about whether or not you **really** deserve the good things that come from self-growth and self-fulfillment, consider the following meditation on ME:

ME

I am the only "me" I've got. I am unique. There are two major parts of me. There is the inside "me" and the outside "me."

The outside me is what you see. The way I act, the image I portray, the way I look and the things I do. The outside me is very important. It is my messenger to the world and much of my outside me is what communicates with you. I value what I have done, the way I look, and what I share with you. The inside "me" knows all my feelings, my secret ideas, and my many hopes and dreams. Sometimes I let you know a little bit about the inside "me" and sometimes it's a very private part of myself.

Even though there are an enormous number of people in this world, no one is exactly like "me." I take full responsibility for "me" and the more I learn about myself, the more responsibility I am going to take. You see, my "me" is my responsibility. As I know myself more and more, I find out that I am an OK person. I've done some good things in life because I am a good person. I have accomplished some things in my life because I am a competent person. I know some special people because I am worth knowing. I celebrate the many things I have done for myself.

I've also made some mistakes. I can learn from them. I have also known some people who did not appreciate me. I do not need to keep those people in my life. I've wasted some precious time. I can make new choices now. As long as I can see, hear, feel, think, change, grow and behave, I have great possibility. I'm going to take those risks and those possibilities, and I am going to grow and love and be and celebrate. I am worth it.

I am worth it!

That's a critical point to bear in mind: All these possibilities, the myriad possibilities of self-fulfillment, entail certain elements of risk. Let's take a closer look at what I mean about the risks of growth.

RISK

Risking is about taking chances. If your life is ever going to change for the better, you'll have to take chances. You'll have to get out of your rut, meet new people, explore new ideas and move along unfamiliar pathways. In a way the risks of self growth involve going into the unknown, into an unfamiliar land where the language is different and customs are different and you have to learn your way around.

Total security is mostly a superstition. It does not exist in nature, nor do the children of men as a whole experience it. Avoiding danger is no safer in the long run than outright exposure. Life is either a daring adventure or nothing.

Helen Keller

When we are ready to grow, we are ready to give up the way we usually see ourselves, which is risky. After all, our old reliable self — no matter how inadequate or unworthy —that's the only sense of self we know. What happens if we lose our old self and *nothing* takes its place? What happens if we obliterate the very essence of our being — our selves?

As we take risks, as we move in the direction of growth, we start taking new "pictures" of ourself, if only in our imagination. We decide we are ready to give up false beliefs, compromises, relationships, poor investments (job, money, energy, volunteer commitments, and so on), superficial attachments and self-destructive habits. Relinquishing these ingrained aspects of our lives can be difficult, but it's absolutely necessary.

Loyalties are often made in the belief that there is safety in groups and in the hope that safety will bring comfort. *However, sometimes it's necessary to leave an institution, a profession, or a group to find individual self-worth and inner comfort.*

In the past, we may have placed energy and resources in friendships that did not flourish. It's time to let go and move on. Clinging to false hopes keeps us from our own growth. In every risk, there is bound to be some loss, something that has to go in order to be able to move ahead. Becoming comfortable with loss is a part of growing.

Some people stay in relationships because they seem secure. Others take and stay in dead-end jobs because they fear new responsibilities. Still others gravitate to groups because they dread being alone. There's an undercurrent of fear that pulses through them incessantly, a message from the scared inner child:

"I am unlovable, I had better settle for what I have, I'd better not take any chances."

Yet the paradox is that until we give up all that feels secure, we can never really trust the friend, mate, or job that offers us something. True personal security does not come from without, it comes from within. When we are really secure, we must place our total trust in our self.

If we reject deliberate risk-taking for self growth, we will inevitably remain trapped in our situation. Or we end up taking a risk unprepared. Either way, we have placed limits on our personal growth, have cut ourselves off from action in the service of high self-worth.

Primarily, what we are talking about here is the risk to be yourself. It seems such a simple thing. We've heard it from childhood: "Just be yourself." Simple, indeed, on the surface, yet no other risk is so fearful and fraught with anxiety.

People who are afraid of being themselves cheat themselves out of finding out what life is all about. To go through life pretending to be something you are not or feel what you really don't is not being real. It's being dishonest, inauthentic, phony. Real prestige and self-worth are not built upon pretense. If you do not risk changing when the time is right, you will probably be forced to change when you are least prepared for it. And the changes may not be healthy ones.

There Is A Time For Giving Up Old Ways of Being and Moving On. The Moment Is Different For Each Person. There Is No Magical Time When Risk Is Easier.
Each Person's Inside Self Knows The "Best" Times.

The risks we must take to attain a more honest life are always more difficult at the beginning. It gets easier as we make choices and changes. As we get comfortable with the habit of risk, it becomes a daily possibility. The life we are creating for ourself becomes limitless and starts looking like a world full of possibilities.

For The Risk-Taker, The World Becomes Full of Possibilities.

Each exercise on the following pages will offer us possibilities, sometimes risky, yet a full choice, for change is available as we walk through the instructions.

Safety Needs

Before we can move into any high self-worth place, it is important for us to ensure our daily living and safety needs.

We need to be safe and comfortable:
Physically
Financially
There are some basic needs that are essential to survival and these needs must be our first priority.

The Basics:

- Sleep — We have all had an experience where we have been sleep-deprived. After a while we cannot think clearly, we become forgetful and irritated. There is no way to work toward self confidence and assurance while we are over-tired, fuzzy-minded and sapped of energy.

- Shelter and Food — Our surroundings and comfort are necessary in order to feel assured inside. Working toward making your living area colorful, restful and pleasant are very important. If you live in a household where there is a great deal of activity and distraction, you should find yourself your own space and make it as soothing and pleasant to you as possible. Again, one cannot grow in self-esteem while living in a crowded, stormy place.

- Financial Security — I'm not talking about lifetime financial security. What I am talking about is the financial security of shelter, food and transportation. These are basic financial needs that must be met before we can begin to look at ways of increasing self-esteem. Many women have suffered assaults on their self-esteem by living in situations where they were unable or unwilling to meet their own basic criteria for survival. It's important for each person to know they can contribute to their own survival and then make decisions in their life with this knowledge fully in mind.

- Orderliness — In a world that is at times chaotic, noisy, fast-paced and seemingly threatening, it is essential that we create a sense of haven in our surroundings. We need to do whatever we need to do to increase the orderliness, comfort and security of the area in which we live. From this place of outer peace, from our personal sanctuary, it becomes easier to get in touch with inner peace.

- Health — Poor health has an impact on our total functioning — physical, mental and spiritual. It's hard to function at our best when we're feverish, in pain, run-down. Infections, bad teeth, chronic pain, headaches —these and other ailments can reduce us very quickly to our basics.

We can't always prevent disease, but we can take clear and decisive steps to maintain our health and prevent accelerated physical deterioration and decrepitude. We can do what we need to do to get our health at peak performance. This is an important part of readying ourselves for higher self-worth. This includes proper weight, diet, smoking abstinence and an evaluation of mood-altering chemicals. (Alcohol and prescription drugs, abstinence from mood-altering recreation drugs.)

THE CHANGES I NEED TO MAKE

Health "Sample"

WHAT	WHEN	HOW
1. Weight Diet	Now	Join Overeaters Anonymous
2. Smoking	In two weeks	Go to treatment
3. Exercise	Now	Walk a mile a day
4. Drugs	Now	Stop
5. Sleep	In one month	Quit second job. Finish school No late night TV

'ME'

WHAT	WHEN	HOW
1. Weight Diet 2. Smoking 3. Exercise 4. Drugs 5. Sleep		

HOME

What do I like?	What do I want to change?
1. Colors	1. Paint bedroom with favorite color
2. Lots of light	2. Change curtains to blinds
3. My use of good music	3. Buy myself a new tape
4. Beauty	4. Buy a fresh flower each week

In addition to The Basics, we all have love needs. While some people consider love to be a luxury, in a sense love needs are themselves as basic as any other need.

Love Needs

Love Definitions —
  Feeling of strong personal attachment
  Affection
  Attachment

Each of us as separate beings seeks to resolve separateness by attachment with others. In the beginning, this "love" was with parents. Later we find relationships all the way through life to meet these attachment needs. Failure to attach results in all kinds of complications. The absence of love has many harmful consequences, ranging from failure to thrive to shortened lifespan, as well as a warped and stunted emotional and psychological existence. Loneliness kills.

There are many ways to get these attachment needs met. There are levels of attachment in addition to the personal attachment of friendship and partnering. Some attachment needs are met through groups and through rituals.

In rituals, people find a sense of comfort by belonging to a church community, a sports team or a certain class. Each of these groups offer places where you can share goals, ideas and common efforts. There can be a feeling of belonging and importance.

On a more interpersonal level, we find a variety of friendships. Fulfilling attachment and love requires the giving and the receiving of care and affection. In giving and receiving, energy is released, and both people feel alive and connected. It does not have to do with sharing objects, it has to do with sharing essence. Who you are is sharing with who someone else is. Both people are enriched and in this enrichment something new is created. It's called a "friendship." Several meaningful friendships are necessary for each person in order to fulfill attachment needs.

Several Meaningful and Honest Friendships Are Necessary For Each Person In Order To Fulfill Attachment Needs.

MY PRESCRIPTION FOR ME

 PRESCRIPTION:

End energy draining friendships now
Add one new friend a month

Repeat as needed

These sustaining friendships can be nourished by periodic acknowledgement of their importance, as in these following letters:

Sample Love Letter To A Friend . . .

Dear Barbara,

This letter of friendship and love is a special one for me to write. The days go by, and very often I'm filled with a thought of you that makes me glad you are my friend. I'm remembering the time I was so angry at work and needed someone to talk to. I felt comfortable calling you. I knew you wouldn't try and get into my business, nor would you blame me. I could count on you to just let me rant and rave and then remind me that this, too, would pass, and that you cared how I felt.

I'm also remembering the night we had dinner at that awful new restaurant in town. It could have been a horrible evening, yet we got to giggling about everything — the food, the waiter, us, the world. It turned out to be such a refreshing emotional night, even though the restaurant was so bad. It's so easy to have a friend like you.

I could go on, but I don't need to. I just want to remind you that I appreciate you and hope our friendship continues to grow over the years.

Thanks for being my friend,

Another Letter To A Child . . .

Dear Bob,

On this your twenty-second birthday, I want to remind you how happy I have been over the years being your mother. I remember the day you were born and my life was never the same again. How we weathered the good times and the hard times. It's not easy being a young person, and it's not easy being a parent. I think the two of us did pretty well.

I remember your hug on Mother's Day, the call that came when I was in the hospital, the many Christmas presents over the years, your smile when I bake chocolate chip cookies, and how proud I am as you made choices in your life. Today you are my special friend and I thank you.

Lots of Love,

Make A List Now . . .

Letters I Want To Write

1.
2.
3.
4.
5.
6.
7.
8.
9.
10.

A True Friend

Friendship occurs when you wish to further the other person's life and he or she wishes to further yours. There is risk involved because the sharing must be honest and deeper than just the niceties and superficial comments. It involves going inside and sharing your feelings, needs, wants, and fears.

Friendship is always a two-way relationship, a give and take. It means taking the time and having the empathy to listen to the feelings, needs, wants and worries of your friend. Each friend accepts responsibility for half of the relationship and each supports the other. Closeness is a hallmark of friendship.

This kind of friendship requires ongoing attention and care.

This kind of friendship is *risky* because it means self-disclosure, exposure, and vulnerability. And it makes demands on you, but also offers great rewards.

The rewards of friendship are those found in virtually any intimate relationship and every true friendship, like every intimate relationship, contributes to self-worth. Now let's take a closer look at the relationship between self-worth and intimacy.

CHAPTER SIX

Intimacy, Commitment and Self-Esteem

Intimacy is a popular topic these days. And when I talk with groups about ways of developing greater self-worth, the question of intimacy always comes up — much more frequently, in fact, than any other subject. Those seeking to enhance self-worth seem to intuitively recognize that intimacy is essential to growth.

"What is intimacy — how do I recognize it?

"How do I know whether I'm ready for it? How do I know if I can handle a truly intimate relationship?

"How can I prepare for it? Can I learn to be more intimate, or is it a special genetic trait and you either got it or you don't?"

These and other questions arise whenever the topic of intimacy comes up. For this reason, I'm including a fairly lengthy statement about what I think intimacy is and how to get it. There is a wonderful bonus to finding true intimacy in one's life. It produces reliable self-esteem on a fairly regular basis.

Intimacy Is Not A Matter of Chance It Is A Matter of Choice

Intimacy can be between friends, between family members, between lovers. The secret of intimacy is simple:

Intimacy Is Available
To Anyone Who Wants To Work For It . . .

The magic of intimacy and the choice of commitment are challenges for young and old alike. They are special interests in the time of recovery from chemical dependency, co-dependency, adult child issues, and personal pain.

Intimacy is a magical word. Many people long for it, songwriters write about it, and couples complain because they do not have it. Rather than a simple definition of intimacy at this point, I would like to establish some ideas about commitment, recovery, fidelity, and work up to an understanding of what intimacy is all about.

INTERMITTENT CLOSENESS

Whatever the components of the magic of intimacy, we have all experienced intermittent times of closeness:

a) The shared hopes and dreams when a baby is born and a child grows.

b) Two people praying or meditating together.

c) Feeling truly understood by someone when a look or a smile tells the whole story.

d) Being close in the warmth of each other's arms after making love.

e) Watching a child perform (sports, dance, art).

f) Feeling an intimacy with a higher power (through nature, a sunset, majestic mountains, pounding ocean waves).

g) Holiday memories (certain food, songs, traditions).

h) Family celebrations.

Intimacy is a by-product of a way of life, a way of relating to life. It takes many components and skills to learn how to experience intimacy.

Fidelity

The first major component is understanding fidelity. Fidelity, according to Webster means:
Careful observance of duty
Discharge of obligations
Loyalty

What many people fail to realize is that spiritually, our first fidelity of loyalty or obligations is to ourself. Fidelity is the awareness one has of one's own integrity. A basic human need is for a person to honor one's potential for survival, growth and celebration and putting ourselves in situations and around people where it can happen. We all know that early recovery is about survival and reclaiming the person inside who has been lost or medicated. Alcoholics, co-dependents, and adult children have come to recognize their child inside who dies a "feeling" death in childhood as feelings and innocence were shut down and abandoned.

Whether integrity or fidelity to self was developed as a child or lost as a child and is now being reclaimed in recovery, one has a set of values that no one can take away nor can anyone impose from the outside. *Our personal integrity comes from integrating our life experiences with our belief systems.* There is a difference between the definition society imposes about fidelity and the integrity that a person develops in order to affirm oneself and be in a position to contribute oneself to someone or something. We cannot give what we do not have. If we don't have ourself, we cannot give ourself in a relationship.

The ability to be "an intimate" requires we have a set of values that match our behavior to our set of values. We need to know how to be "faithful people" to ourselves before we can give ourself to someone else in good faith.

It's important to understand our recovery as we live in these times of changing relationships, changing commitments and changing lifestyles. Let me mention a few facts that are part of the reality we live in:

> "The Jones have gathered to sing 'Happy Birthday' to Junior. There's Dad and his second wife, Mom and her second husband, Junior's two half-brothers from his father's first marriage, his six step-sisters from his mother's previous unions, 100-year-old great grandpa, all six of Junior's current 'Grandparents,' assorted aunts, uncles-in-law and step-cousins. While one robot scoops up the gift wrappings and another blows out the candles, Junior makes a wish . . . he wishes relationships were simpler."

Relationships are becoming more and more complicated. It's growing more essential for us to face some of the realities that exist in the lives of ourselves, those we love, and those we work with. *It seems that the time is over when solutions for relationships can be easily resolved with simple and traditional methods.*

However, no matter what changes lie ahead in technology and human relationships, it seems certain that the human need for love, belonging, affection and intimacy will ensure that relationships will survive. Marriage and coupling may look different on the outside in future times. We will see single parent families, blended families, step-families, gay families and community families. However, it is quite possible that relationships of the future will be stronger and more involved with each other and even less isolated than the people of today if we face and talk about what is happening.

More and more people will not "settle for" non-fulfilling partnerships and friendships. Let's look at what an intimate partnership or friendship consists of: *"It's a choice between any two people making a commitment to each other to share a meaningful lifestyle. A primary commitment includes a sexual component."*

Thus friendship or relationship is built on fidelity — first to self and then a commitment to each other. This commitment includes mutual interest and support and sharing a common vision of life's purpose and how to achieve it. To qualify for this type of friendship or "coupleship," each person must have developed enough self-worth to have the courage, desire and ability to share oneself fully with another person.

RECOVERING RELATIONSHIPS

For the practicing co-dependent, alcoholic and adult child, there has been an historical bankruptcy of what it takes to share oneself with a friend or partner. What needs to be shared is:

... Spontaneous emotion and feelings (We have been taught to shut down feelings and learned to keep them to self)

... Clear thinking (There is a cluttering of the mind with old rules, shoulds, ideas and expectations)

... Physical health (Food, cigarettes, sugar, over-work have been ways that people have tried to salve the inside pain.

... Sexual vulnerability (Control of others and lack of trust has prevented full sexual development)

... Spiritual yearnings (Day to day survival has prevented the time, energy and trust of a relationship to a higher power.)

For too many alcoholics, co-dependents and adult children, early relationships and marriages were made at a time when their inside self was not developed or aware enough to make a full commitment. *One sometimes wakes up in awareness during recovery and finds oneself connected to another without ever having made a clear, "healthy choice."* When that occurs, it is possible that someone is living in one of the following primary situations:

1. Conflict-Ridden Relationship
Conflict is familiar to someone from an unhappy

home. Bickering, coldness, and sarcasm feels normal. After awhile, one sees no problem with fighting and emotional pain. Bickering becomes an acceptable pattern of relating and people living there carry this type of communicating into all their relationships.

2. De-Energized Relationship

For these people, the early days were full of passion and joy. However, with time, these people let outside concerns get in the way of "couple" closeness. In the outer life, they get along okay. They become very involved with children, grandchildren, work, friends or community. Inside, in the privacy of home or bedroom, the passion and closeness is gone. Boredom and resentment flourish.

3. Convenience Relationship

Very similar to the little-energy relationship. Adult children and co-dependents are accustomed to being "willing to settle for", and this relationship was probably always passionless. The partners have been willing to "settle for" companionship rather than passion or intimate sharing. It's a relationship of commonality in professional interests, hobbies, sports, love of children, etc. The dynamic between the partners is primarily platonic. What each of these partnerships is craving is an:

4. Intimate Relationship

The intimate relationship is full of life. Each partner shares both the inside and the outside life. Each individual develops self and then gives the developed and fulfilled self to the others. The relationship is filled with high energy and both have much to give to the other. Tensions and problems are resolved as they occur, as the partners do not want unresolved conflict between them. Couples and families will go to any length spending time, energy and money to resolve conflict and develop closeness because the relationship is that valuable to them. Time together feels safe, warm and exciting.

Often relationships that came together during the active illness of addiction or co-dependency suffer from problems that pre-date the connection or marriage. These specific problems include:

- Lack of trust of others
- Difficulty being honest
- Fear of anger
- Lack of a "feeling language"

These issues brought into the partnership and then increased because of the partnership can cause a "spiritual divorce" long before one admits or faces an actual divorce of the partnership.

SPIRITUAL DIVORCE

A spiritual divorce has the following characteristics:

1. Habitual sadness in the couple — low energy . . .
2. Mutual sentiments of boredom and emptiness . . .
3. Indifference to each other's problems or dreams . . .
4. Frequent coldness or avoidance in sexual encounters . . .
5. Lack of small courtesies and politeness . . .
6. Climate of mutual distrust . . .
7. More confidence in someone outside the coupleship than with each other . . .
8. Communication routine and superficial . . .
9. Frequent feelings of being alone and misunderstood . . .
10. Insults and sarcasm and a discomfort with healthy anger . . .
11. Much avoidance and little confrontation . . .
12. Overbusy and chaotic social or professional life . . .
13. Loss of the capacity for play and joy . . .
14. An atmosphere of the "violence of silence" in the home . . .

In recovery, we find ourselves with serious relationship choices to make. Two of these choices are:

1. *Full Re-commitment To Each Other*

In re-commitment, both partners begin to seriously evaluate the quality of their relationship and make a decision to re-commit to each other and make whatever changes and choices necessary to grow close. Sometimes this includes qualified outside help. Family members and close friends (even counselors) do not qualify as helpers in this regard.

2. *Full Commitment To One's Personal Recovery*

Sometimes people decide they need to work on their own self before they are ready to make any recommitment or commitment to each other or to anyone else. Then they need to face all the consequences of making this decision and again this may take professional care.

CHAPTER SEVEN

Guidelines
To
Developing Intimacy

If one has made the decision to build the quality of the partnership, I offer these guidelines to develop intimacy. They may seem simple, but it isn't always easy to take the time and energy to follow them.

1. *Take time to listen to each other daily* . . . One study reports that the average partner spends only nine minutes a day face to face, eye to eye in conversation. It's necessary to relate directly and not over the noise of a television, radio or from room to room.

2. *Stick with one issue until resolved, and then be done with it* . . . Rehashing the same issues lessens trust and creates new problems. Each time the same issue is brought up, it adds to it the feelings around the non-resolution. It's often old issues and not new problems that destroy trust and love between couples.

3. *Get to the feelings behind the issues* . . . Issues are power struggles. In discussing in-laws, sex, money, and

children, there are most often two sides, and the arguments become revolving door debates. Feelings are real and tend to aid understanding. With understanding, there can be behavior change and forgiveness. Ultimately, with behavior change, healing begins.

4. *Break the no-talk rule.* If something is bothersome, talk about it. It's dishonest to give hints, play games or expect the other person to be a mind-reader.

5. *Set boundaries with children, relatives and friends* . . . Be very clear about how much of your partnership and business you choose to share with them and how much is none of their business. The largest part of "coupleship" business is private and no one else's business. This is a serious and yet frequent barrier to intimacy as chemically dependent families often have little or no experience with healthy boundaries. Too much inappropriate sharing waters down the relationships between any two people, and lessens trust in many situations.

6. *Make a decision to find out and begin to experience what normal, natural and healthy connections feel like* . . . For a person from an alcoholic family, stress, crisis and high intensity is what feels normal and familiar. In developing an intimate close relationship, there will be times of seeming boredom. Not high and not low — just a new experience of non-intensity. Stick with it. The rewards will be different, but will begin to develop. Instead of highs and lows, rushes and despairs, there will be subtle unfamiliar feelings developing. These feelings will be a sense of belonging, comfort, ease and inner peace. In the beginning, one has difficulty recognizing these feelings, and it may feel like boredom, apathy or nothingness. To enjoy comfort, wellness and inner peace takes time.

7. *Some ways to nurture and develop an atmosphere of caring in one's home:*
    a) Write love messages, cards and notes. Stick

them on mirrors, put in dresser drawers or send them to each other through the mail. I call this "mail magic."

b) Touch often, not sexual, just caring. It's a way of letting each other know that you care and are aware of each other.

c) Decide to never fight or bicker over a meal. In studying healthy relationships and families, one consistent behavior they report is that they look forward to mealtime together.

d) Have a special time together to look forward to each day, week, month and year. This is "time-less time". No particular activity and no one else included. It could be a movie, dinner, walk, mini-trip, etc. A good time frame is . . .

An hour a day
A day a week
A week-end a month
A week every six months

8. *Choose lots of ways to have fun.* Make your home a playground rather than a battlefield. Laugh lots, and sometimes be silly . . . it heals!!!

9. *Learn to fight often, constructively and fairly.* Learn to clear the air of tensions and disagreements when they happen. Discuss disagreements in front of others whom you trust and ask for feedback. Move on. Resentments and avoidances suffocate the energy needed for intimacy.

10. *Very importantly, search for meaning outside of the partnership or friendship.* Call it a higher power, call it God, or search for what you want to call it. Seek the source and the "shared journey" will draw you together in intimacy.

SEX, INTIMACY AND SELF-WORTH

Perhaps the greatest myth in regard to intimacy is that it is primarily sexual. Intimacy includes sexuality and sex — but the fulfillment of sex is directly related to the quality of intimacy that precedes physical contact. Very few people come to me telling me that what they want in their relationship is more sex. Most come searching for more intimacy, more caring, more sharing. When they learn more about intimacy, they then naturally want and enjoy more sex.

Intimacy requires full sensual development. This developmental process develops or is retarded early in childhood and then has the potential for continued development or retardation throughout life. Our senses include sight, sound, touch, feelings and intuition.

In recovery, we often have to go back to childhood development and either learn for the first time or re-learn lost or undeveloped skills. *Sensual re-development* is necessary for most recovering people. Being "turned on" to life is a way of preparing ourself to be "turned on" sensually and eventually sexually.

Two major sexual issues common in recovery are sexual impotence for men, and depression, sexual apathy or non-orgasmic response for women.

Potency is related to energy and personal power. Non-orgasmic response and impotence are related to feeling stuck, dominated and afraid. When we are unable to assert ourselves against dominating influences, we feel impotent and passionless. Depression and apathy result from a person feeling that their actions and wishes do not matter — that they are in situations where they cannot influence the happenings in their life. *Impotence, orgasm and desire increase for people who become capable of intimacy and personal power.*

Eroticism can grow richer with time. A deeper knowledge of your partner leads to greater trust. When you know each other in depth, you can refine passion. A deep intimacy can lead to the greatest sex of all. Committed love draws its wonder and mystery from a deeper well than sexual passion.

Another issue that frequently surfaces during recovery is what to do about faithfulness, jealousy and monogamy. Some of the following thoughts are mine, and some are from George Leonard who writes brilliantly on the subject of "High Monogamy."

He says, "Committed love between two people of high self-esteem is both 'giving love' and being capable of 'receiving love'." When this dynamic takes place, both people are transformed. Monogamy is both exciting and full of possibility. The excitement comes not from the discovery of different partners, but with the newness and differentness of a partner that keeps growing and changing.

The chemically dependent or co-dependent person who has made the spiritual decision to turn oneself over to a Higher Power and commit to abstinence knows all about death and rebirth. The person also knows about the energy and freedom unleashed in surrender and commitment. Two people who follow the same path as individuals and then further commit to each other in "coupleship" experience another level of excitement and energy.

These partnerships, however, are not easy to come by. They require partners who both have "high self-worth," both willing to work, and share a common vision. Each needs to celebrate and support self and the other.

If only one person is in a growth time, only that person experiences the discovery of their own beauty and potential. The more we discover self beauty and worth, the less we are willing to waste our potential. If a person is not in a fulfilled and alive relationship, "the temptation to look elsewhere is increased." Data shows us that most people in extramarital affairs or recreational sex feel they "need change" and deserve to be understood and appreciated. They justify "playing around."

In reality, these people are afraid to make significant changes in their personal lives that would offer them more permanent support. The affair becomes more associated with "relief while avoiding changes," rather than risking permanent and honest change in the day-to-day partnership. After the superficial erotic novelty has faded, after all the stories are told, after all sexual fantasies have been explored, then the adventure of transformation through commitment could begin.

But it is precisely at the moment of commitment that many fear the work involved in caring for another. It becomes time to move on, time to "get involved" with another person rather than seeing oneself clearly and working toward increased closeness. Affairs — casual involvements — have to do with avoiding true commitment, true involvement and intimacy. They are signals for changes in a relationship either toward or away from the current situation.

True intimacy is costly as are most items of value. The development of a relationship will cost one's innocence, one's games, one's illusions and one's certainty.

Intimacy is a by-product of close connections. There are different types of connections between people who choose to develop close sharing relationships.

— Friendship connections may include a parent and grown child, two siblings or friends. The criteria for intimacy applies in all meaningful relationships. Intimates care deeply about the way the other looks, feels, thinks, and dreams. So often we hear people say, "I feel closer to my friends than to my family." That is because of the *level of intimacy and sharing they have risked.*

— The primary connection and commitment is to a mate because the mate connection adds the dimension of monogamous sexual dynamics.

— The ultimate connection and commitment is to a higher power. Being truly intimate means to be significant to each other, and to share feelings, thoughts, wishes, fears and dreams.

It is to share pleasure and pain in the safety of trust and commitment, and then to choose experiences, surroundings and friendships and behavior that will enhance the connection to one's self, a partner, and a higher power. One learns carefully to choose people into their life space who:

1. Offer the best possible support for one's growth, changes and striving toward a personal destiny. In

short, one develops a cheering section who cares.

2. It's also important that the people you invite into your life have a vision you can respect and admire so that you can provide a cheering section for them.

Some of you will want several friendships to fulfill your intimacy needs and some of you will want a primary mate. Both choices can fulfill needs and help us each find our destiny. *Intimates are people who help us find our destiny and support us.* They can be partners, parents, our children, or our friends.

CHARACTERISTICS OF INTIMATES

Some of the characteristics of intimates:

1. Intimates fight, laugh, plan, share ideas, and fill the relationship with high energy. ("Fun to be with")

2. Intimates share authority in relationships. They take turns to provide times or situations where they take turns being leader.

3. Intimates accept and appreciate change. They know that change and reality are closely linked, and little remains the same.

4. Intimates can be counted on for consistent behavior. That is how they build trust.

5. Intimates have enough self-worth to know they deserve closeness, care and attention, and don't have to play games for attention.

6. Intimates develop their sense of humor. They save enough money, energy and time to play together, and sometimes do outrageous things.

7. Intimates learn to ask for what they want and need, and give up manipulation and whining.

8. Intimates can become "like children" with each other without embarrassment. Do not waste a day or a night without some appreciation for each other.

Intimacy is a peak experience.

CHAPTER EIGHT

Emotional Needs and Self-Worth

SOME RELATIONSHIPS NEED TO END

While intimacy is a peak experience, not all relationships encourage intimacy. As I pointed out earlier, some relationships are hostile to growth, psychonoxious, physically and emotionally destructive. Others are phantom relationships, existing only as an habitual, dimly felt, dimly perceived presence. Some relationships are conflict-laden, or they're de-energized, or they're simply a matter of convenience.

Now that brings us to a harsh reality, where we strip away the conventional veneer of strained cordiality and look at the core of our relationships. When examined closely, some relationships stand up well. They are solidly founded on the strengths of both parties in the relationship. Many other relationships, however, appear shaky, almost insubstantial at the core.

For example, a good many alcoholics, co-dependents and

adult children, began relationships out of desperation or inertia, without much thought, without healthy choices. They sought a cure for their emotional pain in a relationship with another, only to find themselves not cured, but numbed and in greater distress than before. The reality of those relationships is that one person wants to recover and take responsibility for personal integrity, and the other partner does not.

At this point, we must honestly assess our friendships and primary relationships. Sometimes two people can choose to lead separate lives together, and many times it doesn't work.

Psychiatrist David Viscott once wrote: "There comes a time in some relationships when no matter how sincere the attempt to reconcile the differences or how strong the wish to recreate a part of the past once shared, the struggle becomes so painful that nothing else is felt and the world and all its beauty only add to the discomfort by providing cruel contrast."

A hard truth to meet head on: *Some relationships need to end.*

It often greatly upsets the partnership or other relationships if one person chooses to believe in self. Sheldon Kopp says, "Such people often give the appearance of hyper-normal stability and family or marital goodness." What actually occurs is that they have developed an elaborate system of subtle comments and clues and punishments to warn the other against spontaneity or change, because then the precarious relationship balance would topple and the hypocrisy of the over-controlled pseudo-stability would be exposed.

In couples or families where true consistent pain masquerades as stability and status quo, the struggle in recovery will be to keep the "relationship or family myth going." Individual recovery will be seen as selfish, outrageous, unfair and even weird. Relief in these partnerships or families will then be employed by eating disorders, (especially overweight), return to chemicals, smoking addiction, abuse of prescription medicines, criticism, sarcasm, sexual disinterest or acting out.

If both partners are not willing to take time to work on a committed full partnership, it needs to be recognized that one cannot move in two directions at the same time without internal stress. And that stress causes complications. A measure of how we are valued and loved comes from those standing in our cheering section as we move toward our own growth. If you need to change a commitment, honestly explore your situation. *"True fidelity is a service to the life energy — not a consecration to first commitments or one style of existence. A person faithful to spiritual guidance knows that fidelity unto death does not mean that one does a certain thing until he dies biologically, but only as long as one avoids spiritual death. The faithful person is not the one who maintains first commitments but rather the one who remains committed to life energy at all cost. Face what needs to be faced. That's what reality and fidelity are about."*

Leo Buscaglia outlines the strength of a good relationship in his book *Loving Each Other*:

> The very measure of a good relationship is in how much it encourages optimal intellectual, emotional and spiritual growth. So, if a relationship becomes destructive, endangers our human dignity, prevents us from growing, continually depresses and demoralizes us — and we have done everything we can to prevent its failure — then, unless we are masochists and enjoy misery, we must eventually terminate it. We are not for everyone and everyone is not for us. The question is, "If we cannot be with another, can we at least not hurt them? Can we, at least, find a way to co-exist?"

ON YOUR OWN

Popular advice columnist Ann Landers gives this advice to those who are considering divorce: Decide whether you are better off with or without your mate. Then make your move.

Okay, you've made your move — then what?

Separation is a painful reality that many of us must face in our lifetime. There are two responses that tempt us after a separation:

- Immediate involvement with another — the well-known rebound syndrome in which a person usually gets mired in a relationship that mirrors past history.
- A refusal to risk any new involvement — a withdrawal into the bleak cell of loneliness and emotional isolation.

But there's a third pathway to choose: Seeking a new kind of relationship. Having abandoned attempts to recreate a fantasy past and refusing to settle for a bland, lonely existence, some are now just beginning to understand intimacy. They feel ready to take some risks and form a relationship.

Let me offer the following thoughts, clues to look for in an intimate other:

Intimate Partnerships Are Created By People Who:

1. See beauty in other people. (We don't find perfect people, we choose people, and try to perfect our ability to love and receive love.)
2. Who can define personal values — know what they believe in.
3. Who demonstrate independence rather than dependence in many areas of one's life (financially, emotionally, spiritually).
4. Who know how to develop one's own self-esteem and give as well as take.
5. Who have learned how to accept the reality of how things are rather than how they wish them to be.
6. Have learned to forgive, and know that life is lived forward fueled by the energy of past forgiveness.
7. Who have learned to appreciate what they have to offer — if we don't love self, it's not a pretty package to give as a gift to another.

Intimacy is not a matter of chance, it is a matter of choice and comes to those willing to work for it. From personal experience, let me share that I think it's worth it!!

Some day, after we have mastered the air, the winds, the tides, and gravity, we will harness for God the energies of love. And then for the second time in the history of the world, man will have discovered fire.

Teilhard de Chardin

Success Is A Journey, Not A Destination . . .

Ben Sweetland

All of us want to feel good about ourselves. Very often, the way we feel about ourselves is connected to the things we are able to do. The need for self-esteem is intertwined with feeling as though we are making some important contribution to life. One of the ways we build our own esteem is by developing a productive contribution. Productive means it must fulfill something in us as well as something in the world. We can accomplish great things in terms of products, money or power. But if we just do more and more and more, we might accomplish much, but still remain empty inside.

The kind of productive work I am talking about needs to be work that remains new, fresh and exciting to us. It means that sometimes our productive work is related to our job, sometimes is a hobby, sometimes it's an exploration. But what is important is that it challenges each of us and keeps us excited, and full of energy. When our daily hours are filled with a low energy task, it is even more important to find "other" productive work that keeps our energy flow high.

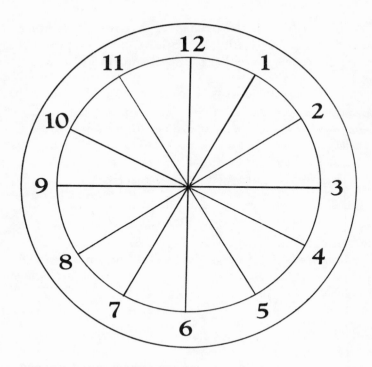

Shade in the hours that are filled with high energy productive work that you like. (Profession, hobbies, tasks). Be sure that the largest number of hours a day are filled with things that are very important to you. If not, what's the next step?

In his book *Self-Renewal*, John W. Gardner noted the importance of "larger objectives" to minimize egocentric tendencies in development (and over-development of the self):

> In the process of growing up the young person frees himself from utter dependence on others. As the process of maturing continues, he must also free himself from the prison of utter self-preoccupation. To do so he need not surrender his individuality. But he must place it in the voluntary service of larger objectives. If something prevents this outcome, then individual autonomy will sour into alienation or egocentrism.

My Creativity

Where	What I Like	What I Want To Change
Job		
Home		
Personally		

RITUALS AND SELF-WORTH

My grandma had a wonderful bit of advice that has brought me much happiness over the years. She told me that she hoped I would follow at least half of the rituals and customs I had picked up in our family. She also challenged me to start or begin at least 50 percent new rituals that started with me. Over the years, I have had fun starting traditions and found them as meaningful as the ones I have followed . . .

Holidays

1. Choosing different dates in December to celebrate Christmas and family relationships, so that on the day of Christmas and Christmas Eve, all family members are able to learn to make their own celebrations. That way many people get their needs met and all the partnerships can choose to be together without worrying about all the parents, children and in-laws. There is plenty of time during that month for family closeness and individual needs.

2. Sunday mornings — My husband and I have chosen Sunday morning to be our special time together. We celebrate it in many ways. However, the ritual is that it is time for just us. No phone calls, no social brunches, no work — just the things we choose to do together.

3. Re-entry time. This is a new one. Both my husband and I lead very busy lives. We find that when we get together after an absence, there is very often a certain amount of tension. This is also true in a milder form at

the end of a day. We now have a ritual that says "stop." Reconnect, reinvest and get acquainted again. It may be a walk, or just going to our cozy sitting room. but we take the time to reconnect the relationship before we put any new stresses on it.

4. A friend a week call . . . It's so easy to get routine and talk to the same people every day. So much wonderful friendship energy is wasted through neglect. Once a week, I choose one friend (local or long distance) and call and say hello, find out how they are, and tell them how I am. It takes very little time (five to ten minutes) and I feel the glow of connection until the next week and the next call.

5. Birthday letters . . . On birthdays of special friends (also children and parents), I write that person a love letter, letting them know how much they mean to me and specifically mention the ways their friendship was important to me in the last year.

EMOTIONAL NEEDS

Each day I will practice becoming aware of what I am feeling. As my awareness sharpens, I will also practice expressing my feelings and then paying attention to the new feelings that occur at the time of expression. I will use my own inner stirrings to guide me in decision-making and in learning to care for myself. My feelings will be my guide . . .

EXCITEMENT! HOPE Curiosity
Guilt Sadness JOY
SILLINESS ANGER HURT

In taking care of myself emotionally, I will finish up all old business. I may finish it in person or I may write a letter, but I will finish the business . . .

Sample Letters (Unfinished Business):

Dear Dad,

    I wish I could have told you this before you died. I was always a little afraid of you. Now that I am older, I see that some of my fear was just the fear of being a small child and some of the fear was very real. I remember some of the times when you spanked me and it really hurt. That only made me more afraid of you. Today I know you were trying to teach me, yet at the time, it felt like you didn't love me.

    I wish we would have had some good talks before you died, but we didn't. I have always felt a little unfinished, so this letter is my way of finishing my business with you. I am sorry I didn't get closer to you and I'm sorry you didn't get closer to me. We might have given each other some good feelings. Today I love myself and will not carry these regrets with me any longer. I loved you and I love myself.

*(Not to be sent, just to put away)   Good-bye

Dear Beth,

    It seems that as sisters we never really talk with each other about very important things. Holidays and family emergencies are about the only time we see each other. Maybe that's the way it will always be. Sometimes I wish we could and would share more and become really good friends. At other times I tell myself that distance and age probably will keep that from ever happening. Yet I just wanted you to know that I think about you, care about you, and find myself needing you from time to time. If you share the same feelings, I'd like to hear from you. If not, I'll accept things just as they are and get on with things.

*(To be sent)   Love and Hugs,

    There may be another category of letters, "Letters I'd like to write to clear up business for myself."

Whatever the letters, it's important to remember that letter writing is for *us*, not to change or to control someone else.

ESTEEM NEEDS

We sometimes talk about low esteem and high esteem as if there were fairly precise self-worth gauges that could measure self-esteem to the nearest gallon or millimeter. It's probably closer to the truth to say that self-esteem flows and ebbs. Just as people sometimes have over-expectations about happiness, believing that happiness should be a constant feeling of high ecstasy, and anything less than that is a tremendous disappointment, so there are people who believe that high self-worth should be a continuous peak experience. Any wavering, faltering, or momentary lapses from this peak — any sense of feeling crummy about oneself, even for a little while — is taken as a personal failure, a cause for alarm, and it confirms our darkest fears — that we are basically, fundamentally and irrevocably No Good.

The message in this book is that we are basically and fundamentally Good. Not perfect, but good. And each day we need to remind ourselves of the best we have going for ourselves. The messages we give to ourselves that affirm our traits and differences are affirmations. They are the opposite of the old rules that used to drag down our self-worth. We need to feed our own self-respect and self-confidence by affirming ourselves at least ten ways each day. The first part of this exercise is to make one long list of the things you like best about yourself . . .

Sample—
    I like my eyes
    I like the way I wake up with energy
    I like my skills in music
    I like the fact that I'm nice to cab drivers and waitresses

I like my sense of humor
I like my body
I like my laugh
I like the fact that I have friends
I like my cooking
I like my independence
I like the way I drive
I like my ways of handling money
I like my Christmas shopping in September

List all the things you like and then transfer them to index cards. Put ten affirmations to a card. Each week tape one card to the bathroom mirror and read them each morning and evening. Change the cards each week. As you develop more and more things you like about yourself, write some new cards.

The Journey

Here goes! I am worth it. I'm committing myself to one year of paying close attention to how I treat myself. Each day I'll write a message of how I feel about myself on that day. I'll do my very best to find something about myself that I like each day. At the end of the year, I will look back and find that not only am I a special worth-while deserving person, but I will be able to feel it.

When my feelings pull me down, I experience low energy 4th class feelings — otherwise known as low self-worth.

Remember these indicators of low self-worth:
1. Eating disorders (overweight, anorexic, etc.)
2. Trouble with relationships (intimacy, commitments, affairs).
3. Physical problems (chronic health issues, impotence, non-orgasmic.)
4. Drug and alcohol misuse.
5. Workaholism and frenetic activity.
6. Smoking.
7. Overspending (credit cards to gambling).
8. Dependency on "other" people (family to gurus).

Ultimately we must stop pretending that there's a magical, effortless way to increase self-esteem. The instant metamorphosis from toad to prince, or from beggar girl to Cinderella, happens only in fairy tales.

While I have placed an emphasis in this book on the importance of coming to terms with emotional hangovers from the past, there are some actions that we can take in the present that will increase the likelihood of strengthening our sense of self-worth.

There Are Three Giant Steps To Take
If We Want To Develop High Self-Worth

1. *Remove the toxic substance or behavior*
2. *Look back and make new choices about old messages and feelings*
3. *Develop new behaviors and feelings that enhance a budding new growth of self-worth*

———————————————— ᴏᴦᴏ ————————————————

Self-Worth Is A Choice, Not A Birthright

S E L F - W O R T H
MEMORIES

Day 1
Day 2
Day 3
Day 4
Day 5
Day 6
Day 7

(Make 51 copies of this page and continue for 365 days.)

References

CHAPTER 1
The Hurried Child, by David Elkind, Addison-Wesley, 1981.

CHAPTER 2
Choicemaking, by Sharon Wegscheider-Cruse, Health Communications, 1985.

Another Chance: Hope and Health For the Alcoholic Family, by Sharon Wegscheider, Science and Behavior Books, Palo Alto, 1981.

CHAPTER 3
Of Course You're Angry, by Gayle Rosellini and Mark Worden, Hazelden, 1985.

On Death and Dying, by Elisabeth Kubler-Ross.

CHAPTER 4
The Romance: A Story of Chemical Dependency, by Joseph R. Cruse, M.D., Nurturing Networks.

Another Chance: Hope and Health For the Alcoholic Family, by Sharon Wegsheider, Science and Behavior Books, Palo Alto, 1981.

See also an article in *Self Magazine*, Feb., 1986: "Calm-Down Foods," by Tom Gallagher. This article contained material from the *Carbohydrate Craver's Diet* by Judith J. Wurtman, research scientist at the Massachusetts Institute of Technology.

CHAPTER 7
High Monogamy, by George Leonard

CHAPTER 8
Self-Renewal, by John W. Gardner, Harper & Row, 1964.

Free To Be Faithful, by Anthony Padajano